STRATEGIC MANAGEMENT

STRATEGIC MANAGEMENT

H. Igor Ansoff

Professor, European Institute for Advanced Studies in Management
and
Professor, Stockholm School of Economics

First published 1979 by
THE MACMILLAN PRESS LTD
London and Basingstoke
Associated companies in Delhi
Dublin Hong Kong Johannesburg Lagos
Melbourne New York Singapore Tokyo

Printed in Great Britain by
LOWE AND BRYDONE PRINTERS LTD
Thetford, Norfolk

British Library Cataloguing in Publication Data

Ansoff, H Igor
  Strategic management
  1. Management
  I. Title
  658   HD31

  ISBN 0–333–19686–4

TO SKIP, FOR THIRTY GLORIOUS YEARS

Contents

1 Introduction

'The man with a method good for purposes of his dominant interests is a pathological case in respect to his wider judgement on the coordination of this method with a more complex experience . . . We have here a colossal example of anti-empirical dogmatism arising from a successful methodology.'

' . . . interplay of thought and practice is the supreme authority'.
Alfred North Whitehead

STATE OF KNOWLEDGE

Our concern in this book is with the behavior of complex organizations in turbulent environments. The current state of knowledge about such organizations can be divided into two parts. One comprises practical technology which offers prescriptions on how organizations *should* behave. The other part consists of theoretical insights which describe why and how organizations *do* behave. The scope and volume of both parts are impressive, but from a viewpoint of a practicing manager, there are still serious gaps in the knowledge.

A major gap is that theory and practical technology are, at best, vaguely related. As a result, the former provides little guidance for the evolution of the latter. Technology progresses either through codification of practical experiences or through *de novo* inventions. When new approaches emerge, there is no basis for *a priori* testing of their validity, nor for defining the limits of their applicability. As a result, technology progresses through fits and starts, by trial and error.

Frequently, when new technology is used in settings to which it is inherently inapplicable, it is the technology and not the misapplication that gets blamed for the failure. A recent example is offered by the criticism of the failure of long-range planning to predict the petroleum crisis — a use for which it is inherently unsuited.

Most available theoretical insights are partial, refracted through the optic of a particular theoretical discipline from which they are derived, be it economics, psychology, sociology, political science, or general systems theory. Such limited optics are adequate when key variables in behavior match those of the observing discipline. But they become inadequate, and even distorting, when the behavior requires a multi-disciplinary explanation.

Most of the current theories deal with average properties of organizations as a class, and not with differences and extremes of behavior. (Note the typical titles: *Behavior Theory of* the *Firm*, *Microeconomic Theory of* the *Firm*, and the common reference to 'organization*s*', in the plural, as if they were all alike.) The search for averages and archetypes is typical of young sciences trying to unravel complexity. But, from the point of view of a practicing manager, averages are secondary to his interest in the extremes: in the reasons for pathologics and for successes.

SCOPE OF THIS BOOK

The aim of this book is to contribute to filling the gaps described above. The major aim is to bridge the gap between theory and practice by providing an explanatory theory which can be helpful both for the evaluation and for the development of practical technology. In natural sciences such explanations go under the name of *applied theory* – an intermediate level of knowledge between pure theory and engineering. Applied theory deals with generic concepts, but in a format and language which is translatable into practical problem-solving.

The subject of this book is complex organizations which exchange goods and/or services with their environment. The process studied is their adaptation to the environment under conditions of environmental turbulence. The theory attempts to answer the following questions:

What are the patterns of organizational behavior in a turbulent environment?
What determines the differences in the behavior?
What factors contribute to success and to failure?
What determines the choice of a particular mode of behavior?

What is the transition process by which organizations move from one mode to another?

Unlike most available theories, this theory is *managerial* in the sense that management is identified and treated as an influential social class within the organization. Management is neither idealized, as in microeconomic theory, nor neglected altogether, as in the bulk of organizational sociology. Instead, a variety of managerial behaviors is treated, ranging from forceful to conservative. This element is essential if the connection to practical technology is to be made visible.

Another essential requirement for an applied theory is to treat a range of organizational behaviors ranging from pathological, which endanger survival, to progressive, which optimize the social utility of the organization. Similarly, different levels of environmental turbulence must be recognized which require different types of response from an organization. In this book these requirements are met through the use of a (somewhat arbitrarily) selected five-point scale of turbulence, the same scale for different types of response, and the same scale for the organizational culture and capability for response. A basic hypothesis of the book is that an organization will be successful if environment, response, culture, and capability match each other.

The theory is *multi-disciplinary* in the sense that it seeks an optic appropriate to the problem and not to a particular scientific discipline. There are two paths to such an optic. One is to attempt an integration of the available disciplinary insights into a coherent whole. The other is to work back from the 'real-world' problem, abstract the features which appear critical to explanation of behavior, and then selectively borrow from theoretical insights which may be available.

The second path is followed in this book because one half of my professional lifetime has been spent as a manager and consultant to managers coping with a variety of turbulent environments. Therefore, I felt that my comparative advantage lay in an understanding of the real-world problem, rather than in a catholic knowledge of the available literature. The key concepts and relationships used in this book are derived from my experience as a manager. Having selected these I reached back to individual disciplines for relevant theoretical concepts.

It turned out that one of the most relevant disciplines was

political science – a subject in which I have the weakest academic background. As a result, on this and other occasions, I have probably borrowed awkwardly, without ability to make proper attributions, and with occasional reinventions of the wheel. I hope that my academic colleagues will forgive these sins and judge the results by the criterion of relevance to reality, and not by the more common criterion of proper attribution to prior work.

Like all theories, the present theory is self-limiting in two senses: the scope of the phenomena treated is limited, and so is the depth to which the phenomena are treated.

The present effort is confined to treating what we shall call the *strategic behavior* of an organization: the process of interaction with the environment, accompanied by a process of changing internal configurations and dynamics. There is another companion behavior called *operating*, which is concerned with the internal resource conversion process in an organization. In this book operating behavior is treated indirectly through the influence it exercises on the strategic behavior, particularly through organizational inertia. Thus the applicability of the present theory is proportional to the relative importance of the strategic behavior to an organization. In strategically stable settings, when the relationship to the environment and the environmental turbulence are both stable, this theory does not apply. Thus the present effort can be said to be complementary to, say, the microeconomic theory or the behavioral theory of the firm, both of which concern themselves with competitive behavior.

In the present effort environmental turbulence and power are shown to be primary influences on strategic behavior. But both are treated in limited depth. They are treated as important exogenous variables: the impact of specified values of these variables on strategic behavior is studied, but the process of determination of these values is not. Thus certain states of environmental turbulence are postulated, but the mechanism by which the environment moves from one to another is not explored – nor is the impact on this movement by the organizations which make up the environment. The relationship with the environment is an open-loop one: the environment impinges on the organization and the organization responds; the manner in which this response affects the environment is not explored.

The power dynamics are treated in a similar manner: certain power structures are postulated and their effect is explored, but, with one exception, the mechanism of power transfer is not treated. This important exception is the case when a strategic crisis induces a change in management.

Another important limitation of the present theory is that it treats each organization as an individual non-cooperative actor *vis-à-vis* its environment. Historically this assumption has been valid for virtually all organizations covered by this theory. But recent social developments, particularly in Europe, have already shown that cooperative actions by various organizations in shaping their environment will occur with increasing frequency.

The above limitations underline the central challenge I encountered in writing this book: the challenge of keeping it up to date in the face of the rapid change in the shape of the strategic problem. Today, *c.* 1977, this problem is significantly different from ten years ago, when my first book on the subject made its appearance. At that time the problem was primarily confined to the commercial linkages of an organization to the environment. These linkages changed slowly, so that adaptation of the internal configuration was not a major problem. The internal power structure, particularly in business, was stable and concentrated in the hands of the management. The socio-political impact of the environment on strategic behavior was minimal.

Today, in addition to commercial linkages, socio-political interaction with the environment and competition for scarce resources have become of major importance. The new conditions of turbulence increasingly require an internal cultural shift. Power is increasingly shared by other groups.

To the best of my ability, I have tried to accommodate these new conditions and provide for developments which I could foresee. But undoubtedly, as in the above example of non-cooperative behavior, future events will further limit the applicability of the present theory.

ANTECEDENTS

In terms of direct lineage this work is related to three prior works. One of these, naturally enough, is my own *Corporate Strategy*, published in 1965. *Corporate Strategy* is a prescriptive logical analysis of how business firms should think through their adaptation to the environment. But even as I wrote it, I realized that there was no relevant body of descriptive theory for testing the *a priori* validity and for predicting conditions under which the prescription will work and conditions when it will fail.

Subsequent experience has shown the importance of this deficiency. The book continues to sell well. But many practical applications of prescriptions similar to mine have come to grief, the spread of strategic planning has been slow, and it is only now, ten years later, that the practice of genuine strategic planning is emerging.

In the interim, naturally enough, observers began to ask questions about the usefulness of the original prescription. My own belief continues to be that the prescription was and remains valid, provided that it is applied in an appropriate organizational climate; and, contrariwise, that strategic planning is going to be rejected when the climate in which it is implanted is wrong.

A number of colleagues and I have offered a prescription for matching the climate to strategic planning in a recent book *From Strategic Planning to Strategic Management*, which appeared in 1976. For the past ten years, while working to make strategic planning more applicable, I have also been working on an explanatory theory against which prescriptions for various aspects of strategic management could be tested. This book is a culmination of this work.

For the second parent, I take *Behavioral Theory of the Firm* by Cyert and March, which is probably the most important effort to date to construct a multi-disciplinary theory of managerial behavior. This book differs from Cyert and March in several respects. As already mentioned, they treat the operating problem, whereas we deal with the strategic. They focus on the business firm, whereas our concern is with a larger class of environment-serving organizations. They deal with the conservative firms, while we treat a range from conservative to aggressive organizations. They postulate a single mode of behavior, while we explore a range of behaviors. The environment they study can be predicted by a smooth extrapolation, whereas this book treats both extrapolative and discontinuous environments, as well as environments in which the levels of turbulence change over time.

The third parent is *Strategy and Structure* by A. D. Chandler, which ushered in a new perception of the relationship between a firm and its environment. Chandler's work is based on historical analysis. This book is theoretical, offering predictive hypotheses.

This book, like Chandler's, is built on the basic hypothesis that environment, external strategic behavior, and the internal 'structure' are interrelated.

Over the years, a number of people have given me important insights, which in one way or another influenced this book. Among these are Russell Ackoff, Peter Broden, Derek F. Channon, Ian Clark, Pierre Davous, Roger Declerck, Claude Faucheux Bo Hedberg, Roger Hickman, Les Metcalf, Henry Mintzberg, Andrew Pettigrew, Bengt Stymne, Pierre Tabatoni, and Philippe de Woot. I also owe an important debt to my many friends and fellow researchers in the European 'club' for research on strategic management.

Manuscript preparation has been handled by four persons who have enthusiastically gone way beyond their normal roles in improving this text. They are Ned Sickle and Les Wuescher, who edited the manuscript, Peggy Phelps, who prepared its early versions, and Jessie Goveas, who prepared the final versions.

My greatest debt of all is to my wife Skip, who encouraged and survived many hours of morning 'pillow talk', when key insights and concepts were hammered out.

2 The Overall Framework

'A theory need not give us answers, but it should, perhaps, question the questions until they bleed a little.'

Paraphrased from Anthony Boucher

ENVIRONMENT-SERVING ORGANIZATIONS

The keystone of modern industrial society is a large number of organizations whose principal occupation is to supply goods and/or services to their environment. In capitalist industrialized societies such organizations have been usually grouped into two major categories. One contains 'for-profit' business firms whose assets are owned by private individuals. The other is composed of 'not-for-profits' whose assets are publicly owned. Historically it has been assumed that the respective categories exhibit significantly different non-overlapping behaviors.

The firms were seen primarily as good producers, internally efficient, externally entrepreneurial and aggressive, and committed to a single-minded pursuit of profits. The publicly owned organizations were seen as providing services and their behavior as internally bureaucratic, inefficient, and externally unadventurous. The objectives of profit and efficiency of the business firm were replaced in the not-for-profits by a vaguer concept of rendering 'public service'.

Today, the distinction between the two categories is becoming increasingly vague. Studies of business firms have shown that commitment to maximum profit is, at best, to be found in a minority of firms. The majority exhibits, in various degrees, elements of bureaucratic behavior previously imputed to the nonprofits. On the other hand, the non-profits have on occasion exhibited miracles of efficiency and aggressiveness, as exemplified by Project Apollo.

Just as stereotypes of behavior are overlapping, so are the

8

expectations from the two categories. The 'private sector' is increasingly under pressure to curb its profit-seeking behavior whenever such behavior violates social ethics, or brings about undesirable physical and social 'pollution' side-effects. At the same time, private enterprise is urged to serve the public through inherently non-profitable activities.

In the public sector, as society confronts new problems of education, health, social services, transportation, ecology, use of space, the non-profit organizations are becoming increasingly engaged in entrepreneurial, environment-opening work which was previously reserved for the business firm. At the same time, as government budgets grow and consume an increasing share of the Gross National Product, the inherent economic inefficiency of the non-profits has become overwhelmingly obvious. As a result the public sector is under growing pressure to emulate the efficiency of the business firm.

The growing complexity of society's work and the changing social values have led to a recognition that historical organizational forms are no longer adequate for meeting society's needs. In Europe this has led to modifications in the status of the firm, ranging from the nationalization of assets in Britain, to the public and worker participation in strategic decisions in Germany, to the recent 'full consultation' law in Sweden. In the United States much organizational experimentation has focused on giving a 'business flavor' to publicly owned institutions through creation of so-called 'intersect' organizations. Examples are the Tennessee Valley Authority, the New York Port Authority, Comsat (corporation for management of satellite communications), Amtrak (a government corporation for the management of passenger transport in the north-east corridor of the United States), the New York Post Office and the energy corporation proposed by the Ford administration. Each of these is a hybrid of 'public' and 'private' features. For example, both the publicly owned Post Office and Amtrak have been given a formal 'for-profit' status.

Thus it appears that the distinction between 'private for-profit' vs 'public not-for-profit' organizations is inadequate, either for explaining behavior, or for designing new socially responsive forms.

In this book, we shall treat firms and non-profits jointly as members of a class of organization which we shall call *environment serving*. These are organizations whose primary function is to supply goods and/or services to society. Other writers have called such organizations 'purposive' or 'purposeful', for the obvious reason that their goods production process is a joint purposeful activity of its members. As we shall discuss in detail, the 'purposiveness' of such organizations varies widely, ranging from aggressive optimization to passive maintenance of the status quo. For this reason, the term 'environment-serving' appears as a more appropriate name for the class. For brevity we shall refer to the members of this class as *ESOs*.

Throughout the book, we shall be seeking to identify features which are common to all ESOs and features which distinguish them from one another. We shall find that, at the extremes, the firm and the non-profit are clearly different from one another. But we shall also find a great deal of overlap in the middle range of the common variables. We shall also find that the current societal trend is to increase this overlap.

The class of ESOs includes the business firm, the hospital, the university, the church, and services rendering branches of the government, such as the post office, or an automotive licence registration bureau. In today's society, organizations of this type employ a majority of the work force. Excluded from the class are organizations such as informal social clubs, and legislative, judicial and regulatory branches of the government which have no concrete product or service addressed to outside customers.

ESOs are what in physics would be called 'conservative organizations'. In producing goods and services they consume resources: physical inventory, money, time of the executives. Unless the resources are replenished continuously, an ESO 'winds down' and goes out of business – a condition called bankruptcy in business language.

The replenishment comes from two sources: *commercial* transactions with the environment, in which the output is sold to customers, and *subsidy* transactions, in which certain external agents grant resources to the ESO without requiring a tangible return.

The classical business firm is distinctive among ESOs in its total dependence on commercial transactions. But some firms today (such as publicly owned corporations) share with the not-for-profits the characteristic of partial market dependence. Their commercial transactions are conducted at a deficit, which is made up by grants from the government.

We now state a basic hypothesis which unites the ESO into a distinctive class. Many of the later deductions will be directly traceable back to this hypothesis.

HYPOTHESIS 2.1: SURVIVAL DRIVE
When any ESO is confronted with the prospects of extinction, it focuses all of its energy on a search for a survival strategy.

The survival drive has psychological, sociological and systemic roots. It reflects the individual's drive for personal security, the tribal interdependence and allegiance of social groups, and the inertial tendency of complex bureaucratic systems to continue functioning in a previously established mode.

In the absence of a survival threat, ESOs exhibit a wide range of differences in their interaction with the environment: some (the classicial business firm) seek to maximize their net resources through commercial transactions, others (the predominant number of 'real-world' firms) are consistent seekers of a positive exchange, while still others (the typical not-for-profits) depend largely on subsidies and incur a chronic deficit in their commercial transactions. We shall argue that, among other factors, the relative dependence on commercial or subsidy income has an important influence on the apparent ambitiousness of the ESO, certainly a greater influence than, say, its legal, for-profit status.

THE WORK OF ESOS

The commercial work of an ESO can be divided into three distinctive categories:

1. *Entrepreneurial* work concerned with divesting from obsolete products/services; creating new products/services, identifying customers for them, finding ways to make the products attractive to the potential customers, and establishing the new products/services on the market;
2. *Operations* work concerned with converting input resources into finished products/services;
3. *Marketing* work concerned with selling and delivery of the products/services to the customers.

The operations work is introverted, focused on the inner workings and efficiency of the ESO. The entrepreneurial and marketing work, although performed 'inside' in the sense that it is done my individuals belonging to the organizations, is extroverted. The important transactions take place either directly in the environment (such as selling), or with major awareness of the needs of the environment (such as development of new products). We shall jointly call entrepreneurial and marketing work the *strategic work* of the ESO.

The classification of entrepreneurial, operations and marketing work is equally applicable to the subsidy interactions with the environment. For example, a federal agency seeking a subsidy will first engage in developing a proposal which is attractive to the grantor; then it will engage in a proposal-selling effort of influencing the right officials and anticipating moves by competitive bidders; and, having secured the grant, it will focus on administering it.

The same classification of work is equally applicable to a third important type of transaction between the ESO and its environment. These are *political* transactions which legitimize an ESOs position in society:

1. *Entrepreneurial* political work is concerned with identifying the purpose of the ESOs existence (its *raison d'être*), as well as the freedoms and constraints under which it shall operate (the *rules of the game*), and negotiating the *raison d'être* and the rules of the game with the powerful members of the ESOs environment. In the language of politics entrepreneurial work is called 'statesmanship'.
2. *Marketing* political work consists in maintaining and promoting social activity (such as laws, public attitudes) which are consistent with the desired *raison d'être* and the rules of the game. In the United States political marketing is called 'lobbying or public relations'.
3. *Operating* political work consists of developing the information and other materials essential for the marketing activity.

Prior to the 1950s and for the preceding hundred and fifty years, the *raison d'être* for both the firm and non-profit ESO remained clear and stable. Non-profits were limited to performing social services, which were inherently non-profitable. The business firm was expected to build national wealth and provide goods and services in all areas of social need where profit could be made. The rules of the game typically limited the activity of non-profits to the scope defined in their charter. They were expected to operate at a deficit, which was to be covered by governmental subsidies, or charitable contributions. The basic rule of the game for the firm, founded on Adam Smith's philosophy, was *laissez-faire* — an unrestricted freedom to compete and a freedom to engage in any commercial activity the firm wished to undertake.

The clarity of the terms of reference eliminated any need for political entrepreneurial activity. It also eliminated a need for political marketing by the non-profits. However, starting in the second half of the nineteenth century, literal application of *laissez-faire* doctrine to the firm produced a number of socially undesirable side-effects. As a result, society began increasingly to place constraints on the behaviour of the firm, some designed to limit the side-effects and some to preserve competition. In response, firms, singly and jointly through various associations, typically increasingly engaged in political marketing (lobbying), seeking to defend the concept of the 'free enterprise'.

During the second half of the twentieth century, the situation began to change drastically. As we shall be discussing presently, not only the rules of the game but also the *raison d'être* is being questioned and changed for both the firms and the non-profits. As a result, it is safe to predict that ESOs will increasingly engage in both political entrepreneurial and marketing activity.

The preceding discussion identified two dimensions of organizational activity: the type of transaction with the environment, and the kind of work performed by the ESO. These are summarized in Fig. 2.1 where the cross-hatched area indicates the self-imposed limits of this book. *Our concern will be limited to the commercial strategic behavior of ESOs, including both the entrepreneurial and the marketing aspects.*

But, clearly, commercial strategic behavior cannot be taken in isolation, since it interacts with the other cells of the figure. In the present work, we shall treat these interactions as exogenous influences on the strategic behavior. Thus, as shown in the figure, the influence of the operating work is accommodated through its impact on the ESOs strategic culture and organizational inertia. The influence of the political transactions is felt through the

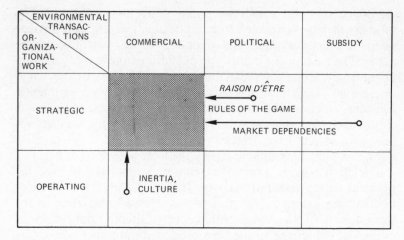

ENVIRONMENTAL TRANSAC- TIONS / OR- GANIZA- TIONAL WORK	COMMERCIAL	POLITICAL	SUBSIDY
STRATEGIC		*RAISON D'ÊTRE* RULES OF THE GAME MARKET DEPENDENCIES	
OPERATING	INERTIA, CULTURE		

Figure 2.1   Scope of the Book

politically imposed *raison d'être* and the rules of the game.

The total income of an ESO is made up of the contributions made by the commercial and the subsidy transactions. The higher the subsidy income the less income has to be gained from commercial activity. We shall use the dependence of an ESO on its commercial market as a measure of the influence of subsidy transactions on the commercial activity.

From the viewpoint of society, the effectiveness of an ESOs commercial activity, for both firms and non-profits, can be measured by two complementary criteria: (1) The degree to which the ESOs products/services respond to the needs of its customers; and (2) the efficiency with which the ESO uses resources in supplying these needs.

An underlying assumption of the microeconomic theory is that, under conditions of perfect competition, when numerous competitors are left unrestrained to compete for the favor of customers, both criteria will be optimized simultaneously: the customer will be best served and the firm will gain maximum profit.

But perfect competition is seldom observable and in most situations the two criteria are not optimized simultaneously. Many firms seek profits through satisfying the customer, but many others seek to influence him into buying what the firm wants to sell, even to the extent of concealing the true characteristics of the product. A majority of non-profits pay little attention to either of the above criteria: they are neither responsive to customers nor economically efficient.

Thus, for the purposes of the study, we need a basic assumption which is somewhat broader than that of the microeconomic one. We should assume *first, that many firms and all non-profits do not seek to optimize their economic efficiency; second that both optimizers and non-optimizers concern themselves with the welfare of the customer only to the extent that it serves their internal economic aspiration. In other words, environment-serving organizations are selfish and not altruistic.*

For purposes of comparison of behaviors and assessment of survival prospects we shall measure economic effectiveness by the ratio of the net return to an ESO from its commercial transactions divided by the resources employed by the ESO:

$$\text{ROI} = \frac{(\text{Income from commercial transactions}) - (\text{Costs incurred})}{\text{Resources Employed}}$$

where ROI stands for 'return on investment'.

ROI is a commonly used key objective in the business firm. But it is not the only objective used by firms, nor is it an objective in the behavior of non-profits. Therefore, our use of ROI will not be as imputed objective, but as a yard-stick of comparison, as an indicator of relative social efficiency in the use of the resources invested in the ESO. It is safe to predict that the enormous and growing social investment will lead eventually to adoption of an ROI-like concept in the management of non-profit ESOs.

MULTIPLE POWER CENTERS

Within an ESO there is typically a division of work between two classes of individuals. One of these, usually called 'managers' in the firm and 'administrators' in the not-for-profits, does not do any actual resource-conversion work. This group's sole pre-occupation is with guiding and controlling the behavior of the organization. In the words of modern German and Dutch terminology, these are the 'work-givers' – the individuals who are engaged in determining what is to be done, in inspiring and motivating others to do it, and in controlling the results. The work-givers guide organizations through a combination of two distinctive tools: (1) *personal leadership* applied through power, example, persuasion and inspiration; and (2) *systems, structures* and *procedures* which enforce a certain *performance discipline* in the conduct of ESO activity.

The tradition decrees that work-giving managers in the business firms are typically more aggressive and ambitious than their counterpart administrators in the not-for-profits. Studies of managerial behavior and common observation show the picture to be more complex. The hard drivers *are* found typically, but not exclusively, in some business firms, but a variety of weaker managerial behaviors can be observed in a majority of firms and in practically all of the not-for-profits.

In the early days of the business firms (and in small business firms today) management was a small, closely knit group, usually composed of the owners of the enterprise. Today, in most firms and non-profits the management group is large and non-homogeneous. Typically, as one descends through the managerial hierarchy, the allegiance of the managers to the purpose of the enterprise decreases, and personal aspirations and ambitions become increasingly strong motivators of behavior. Lower-level managers also see the purpose of the enterprise from the typical parochial perspective of the functional activity which they represent and typically feel that the welfare of the enterprise will be optimized through optimization of performance in their particular area. As a result, the influence of management on strategic behavior is not a monolithic force, but rather a conglomeration of frequently opposing and contradictory forces.

A second class of individuals in the ESO are the 'work-receivers' – both blue and white collar workers, who are engaged in the actual processes of resource acquisition, conversion and product disposal. They are the indispensable component of strategic work, because without them ESO activity would be confined to unimplemented plans and intentions.

In modern industrial culture (with the exception of Japan) the work-receivers typically feel no responsibility for the economic success of the enterprise, and bring to their work aspirations personal economic well-being and fulfillment. Just as managers, work-takers are not a homogeneous group and tend to organize themselves according to professional skills.

Thus in a modern ESO a number of actors and groups of actors have distinctive aspirations for strategic behavior. *A central assumption of this book is that these aspirations influence the choice of behavior as a function of the power possessed by the various aspirants and the power dynamics among them.*

As we shall be discussing in detail later, in the business firm power was originally concentrated in the hands of the owners. By the middle of the century power had passed into the hands of the managers. Since then the work-receivers have been progressively accumulating power, partly through control of technological knowhow and partly through legal modifications in the power structure (evident in Europe). The trend in the firm is thus toward the power structure found in most non-profits, where work-receiving technocracy has traditionally been strong and management relatively weak. Thus, increasingly, strategic behavior is determined through interaction of multiple power centers, each of which seeks to impress its own set of aspirations of the ESO.

OVERVIEW OF THE MODEL

A central concept of the proposed theory is that the commercial results realized by an ESO are largely determined by an alignment of certain attributes. This concept is an extension and elaboration of Chandler's strategy-structure hypothesis. Part of this alignment is external between the level of environmental turbulence and what we shall call the *strategic thrust* of the ESO. Another part is internal between the strategic thrust and three attributes of the ESO: its *strategic culture*, its *managerial capability*, and its *logistic capability*.

To diagnose the alignment, we shall construct a scale of environmental turbulence and then matching scales for each of the above attributes. When the attributes are properly matched, the potential performance is optimized; when they are not, the potential deteriorates proportionally to the mismatch.

The performance is also influenced by the resource commitment, the *strategic budget*, which the ESO makes to its strategic thrust. The theory defines for each environment a strategic budget level, called *critical mass*, below which the ESO cannot hope to realize a positive net commercial exchange with the environment. Above the critical mass the ROI rises for a while as budget is increased, but eventually levels at a maximum.

The performance is also influenced by the personal *performance drive* of the managers and by the *power* available to them for translating this drive into the performance pressures they put on the ESO.

In addition to performance, the theory is concerned with the process by which an ESO chooses its strategic thrust. This process is modelled in Figure 2.2. The *market dynamics* model matches the ESOs strategic behavior to the environmental turbulence to produce the economic results. The results become known inside the ESO through its accounting system. For some ESOs, this is the only information used by management. But for many others additional information is obtained directly from the environment.

The obtaining of this information is modelled in the *perception of the environment*. The model is based on an interaction between the information gathering mechanism (which is a part of the *managerial capability* shown in the lower right-hand box) and by the openness of the managerial *culture* to information which departs from past. Both mechanisms produce an internal perception which may or may not correspond to the outside reality.

The perceived prospects are one of the inputs which determine the levels of performance to which the ESO aspires in the model. The other key factors which determine the aspirations are: the historical tradition and inertia, the self-serving aspirations of powerful groups and individuals, and the managerial aspirations of the strategic leadership which seeks to optimize the organizational rationality.

As treated in the model, the aspirations formation process may or may not be explicit. In many firms and some non-profits, the process is formalized under the name of goal-setting, and is conducted through a management system such as budgeting, MBO (management by objectives), long-range planning, or strategic planning. But in most non-profits and also some firms, the process of aspiration formations is implicit, heavily political, and indistinguishable from the process of strategic choice. Put differently, in 'rational' ESOs the objectives are formed explicitly through a rational-political process and then the strategic choice is made according to the agreed objectives. In 'political' organizations, on the other hand, political bargaining is typically about strategic choice and the aspirations are not negotiated.

As shown in Figure 2.2, the choice of aspirations interacts with

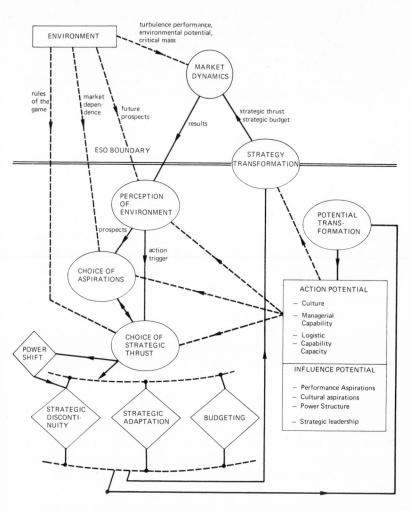

Figure 2.2 Model of ESO Behavior

the model of *choice of strategic behavior*. The model of the strategic choice is similar to the choice of aspirations in the fact that it is determined by historical, political and managerial influences. Additional important influence is exerted by the environment: the rules of the game delimit the range of feasible strategic choice, and the level of turbulence delimits the modes of strategic behavior which can produce the desired aspirations. An important point, which will be developed later, is that in many ESOs the chosen strategic mode is not consistent with the chosen aspirations, resulting in suboptimal behavior.

The four rhombuses shown at the bottom of Figure 2.2 make up a schematic diagram of alternative strategic choices which an ESO makes. As the three lower rhombuses show, the model provides for three alternatives: *budgeting behavior* during which there is no strategic change, strategic adaptation which is consistent with past strategic changes of the ESO, and *strategic discontinuity* which breaks with past experience. Frequently, before embarking on a discontinuity, ESOs undergo a transfer of controlling power as shown in *power shift*. In the closing chapter of the book, we shall explore in detail the mechanism of transition in strategic behavior.

The square boxes at the lower right of Figure 2.2 group the principal forces which, as the dotted lines show, affect each step in the strategic behavior process. One group, the *action potential*, represents passive forces which affect the outcomes and the course of action. The other group, the *influence potential*, represents the triggering forces which affect the choice of behavior.

Complex as the overall model may appear from Figure 2.2, the exploration of the model becomes even more complex as we attempt to deal with a range of possible combinations. We shall be dealing with five distinctive environments, five types of strategic thrust, five different cultures, five types of competence, three types of power structure, three modes of strategic behavior and two types of strategic leadership – a total of 11250 combinations. Developing a way to write about this many combinations without losing myself or the reader in a welter of incomprehensible complexity has been a major learning experience for me, and also the reason why this book has been rewritten four times. I am hopeful that this fourth version will prove readable with a modest amount of effort.

3 The Environment in a Historical Perspective

'The problems of the U.S. economy have an unnerving tendency to be something different today from what you thought they were yesterday.'

Carol J. Loomis

'Trend is not destiny.'

René Dubois

THE INDUSTRIAL REVOLUTION

Modern business history in the United States starts roughly in the 1820s and 1830s. First the construction of a network of canals, and then of a nationwide railroad system triggered a process of economic unification of the country. A stream of basic inventions – the steam engine, the cotton gin, the Bessemer steel process, the vulcanization of rubber – provided a technological base for a rapid industrial takeoff. Technological invention proceeded alongside social invention and the development of one of the most successful and influential organizations in history – the business firm.

By 1880–1900 a modern industrial infrastructure was in place. It unified the country into an American common market. The firm emerged as a privileged and central instrument of social progress. This period in the U.S., which became known as the 'industrial revolution', was one of extraordinary strategic turbulence. The early industrial entrepreneurs devoted most of their energies to creating modern production technology, surrounding it with organizational technology, and staking out their market shares. The concept of competition, as it is known today, did not begin to evolve until the 1880s. The earlier concept was to

21

dominate or absorb the competitor rather than meet him head-on on the market place. Modern marketing, as we know it today, was yet to be developed.

THE MASS-PRODUCTION ERA

From 1900 on, the focus shifted to developing and consolidating the industrial structure created during the Industrial Revolution. This new period, which lasted until the 1930s, has been named the 'mass-production era' and, as the name suggests, the focus of industrial activity was on elaborating and perfecting the mechanism of mass production which progressively decreased the unit cost of products. The concept of marketing was straightforward and simple: the firm which offered a standard product at the lowest price was going to win. This was succinctly summarized in the phrase of Henry Ford I, who, in response to a suggestion in favor of product differentiation, responded to his sales people: 'Give it (the Model T) to them any color so long as it is black.'

There were many problems to be solved, but worrying about strategic challenges was not one of them. The industrial lines were well drawn and most industries offered promising opportunities. The inducement to diversify into new environments appealed only to the most adventurous firms. A majority were satisfied with their own growth prospects. It was obvious that the steel companies were in the 'steel industry', automobile companies were in the 'automotive industry'. As a result managerial attention was focused inward on the efficiency of the productive mechanism. The result was a set of managerial perceptions, attitudes and preferences which later came to be known as 'production mentality'.

On the political front, the business sector was well protected against outside interference. Political and social controls were minimal. Government 'interference' with the free enterprise was infrequent. When needed, the government could be expected to provide a protectionist economic policy. When business flagrantly transgressed social norms, government reacted by limiting freedoms of business action, such as by anti-trust or anti-price collusion legislation. But these were occasional events; most of the time the boundary of the business environment remained inviolate. The business of the country was business. It was this sense of the centrality of the business sector that led 'Engine Charlie' Wilson, a president of General Motors, to say: 'What is good for General Motors is good for the country.'

THE MASS-MARKETING ERA

For the first thirty years of the century, success went to the firm with the lowest price. Products were largely undifferentiated and the ability to produce at the lowest unit cost was the secret to success. But toward the 1930s the demand for basic consumer goods was on the way toward saturation. With 'a car in every garage and a chicken in every pot' the increasingly affluent consumer began to look for more than basic performance. Demand for the Model-T type of product began to flag.

In the early 1930s General Motors triggered a shift from production to a market mentality. The introduction of the annual model change was symbolic of a shift from standard to differentiated products. By contrast to the earlier 'production orientation', the new secret to success began to shift to a 'marketing orientation'. Mr Ford, having tried to replace a standard Model T with a standard Model A, was forced to follow the multi-model suit of General Motors. Promotion, advertising, selling and other forms of consumer influence became priority concerns of management.

The shift to the marketing orientation meant a shift from an internally focused, introverted perspective to an open, extroverted one. It also meant a transfer of power from production-minded to marketing-minded managers. Internal conflict and power struggle were a frequent outcome. But, beyond power struggle, managers resisted the shift because it required costly, time-consuming and psychologically threatening acquisition of new skills and facilities, development of new problem-solving approaches, changes in structure, in systems and acceptance of new levels of uncertainty about the future.

In process industries and in producer-durable industries, the marketing concept was slow to penetrate. When confronted with saturation, firms in such industries frequently settled for reduced growth under production orientation, rather than undertake the pains of a shift to the marketing outlook. It was not until after World War Two that many of these industries were propelled by new technologies, first into a belated marketing orientation, and soon thereafter into the higher turbulence of the post-industrial era.

Consumer industries and technologically-intensive producer industries were early in embracing the marketing orientation. An overswing frequently occurred: marketing began to dominate operations at the expense of the production efficiency. As a compensation for the overswing, a 'total marketing concept' emerged which balanced the conflicting demands of marketing and production. Such balanced sharing of priorities gradually emerged and is still to be found in most progressive firms.

The mass-production era greatly enhanced the marketing turbulence of the environment. The enterprise-changing strategic activity, which subsided during the mass-production period was also enhanced, but less drastically. In technology-based industries, new product development became an important activity early in the century. An historical milestone was the establishment of intra-firm research and development laboratories in companies such as Du Pont, Bell Telephone and General Electric, a step which institutionalized innovation within the firm.

In low-technology consumer industries the advent of the annual model change generated a demand for incremental product improvements, better packaging, cosmetic appeal, etc. But, with significant exceptions, the change in products and markets was evolutionary, rather than revolutionary. Focus on current markets and products dominated the concern with future profit potential.

During the industrial era most of the major changes in the environment originated from leading aggressive firms which established the style and the pace of progress. Thus, with considerable justification, business could claim to control its own destiny. To be sure, business initiative sometimes produced an invisible chain of adverse consequences which led to periodic 'loss of control', such as recurring recessions. But these were viewed as the price of competitive freedom well worth paying for a 'blowing off' of 'economic steam' to enable progress to resume. These periodic 'suprises' were seen as an exception in an otherwise surprise-free world.

TRANSITION TO THE POST-INDUSTRIAL ERA

From mid-1950 accelerating and cumulating events began to change the boundaries, the structure and the dynamics of the business environment. Firms were increasingly confronted with novel unexpected challenges which were so far-reaching that Peter Drucker called the new era an 'Age of Discontinuity'. Daniel Bell labelled it the 'post-industrial era' – a term we shall adopt for our discussion. Today, change continues at a pace which makes it safe to predict that the current escalation of turbulence will persist for at least another 10–15 years. It is also safe to predict that, as in other epochs in history, today's turbulence will turn out to be a symptom of society's transition to a new set of values and structures. It is harder to predict when society will begin to settle down once again to absorbing and exploiting the accumulated change. Thus the current period is better labelled as a period of transition to the post-industrial era.

To an outside observer, business problems of the mass-production and mass-marketing periods would appear simple by comparison to the new turbulence. The manager's undivided attention was on 'the business of business'. He had a willing pool of labor (so long as the wage was right), and he catered to a receptive consumer. He was only secondarily troubled by such esoteric problems as tariffs, monetary exchange rates, differential inflation rates, cultural differences, and political barriers between markets. Research and development was a controlable tool for increased productivity and product improvement. Society and government, though increasingly on guard against monopolistic tendencies and competitive collusion, were essentially friendly partners in promoting economic progress.

But managers who worked inside firms during the earlier periods had found the problems of the era very complex, challenging and demanding. Outside the firm, the manager had to fight constantly for market share, anticipate customers' needs, provide timely delivery, produce superior products, price them competitively, and assure the retention of customer loyalty. Internally, he had to struggle constantly for increased pro-ductivity through better planning, more efficient organization of work, and automation of production. Continually he had to contend with union demands and still maintain the level of productivity, retain his competitive position on the market, pay confidence-inspiriting dividends to stockholders, and generate sufficient retained earnings to meet the company's growth needs.

It was natural, therefore, for a busy manager initially to treat the Post-Industrial signs in much the same way he had treated periodic economic recessions. Inflation, growing governmental constraints, dissatisfaction of consumers, invasion by foreign competitors, technological breakthroughs, changing work attitudes – each of these changes was at first treated as a distraction from 'the business of business' to be weathered and overcome in the expectation of a return to a focus on marketing and operations.

As a result, just as in the earlier shift from production to the marketing orientation, the shift to a post-industrial orientation is slow and still resisted in many firms, because it introduces new uncertainties, threatens a loss of power, requires new perceptions and new skills. The resistance to change frequently leads to a gap between the behavior of a firm and the imperatives of the environment. The firm continues to focus on marketing and disregards the technological and political changes; it continues to rely on past precedents, when experience is no longer a reliable guide to the future. Managerial attitudes are well summed up by a popular French saying: *'Plus ça change, plus c'est la même chose.'*

But it is not *'la même chose'*. The basic cause of the new turbulence is the arrival of economic affluence. The mass-production era was a drive to meet the basic physical comfort and safety needs of the population. The mass-marketing era lifted the aspirations from comfort and safety to a drive for affluence. The post-industrial era is the arrival of affluence.

Satisfaction of survival needs and the parallel growth in discretionary buying power change consumer demand patterns. Industries that served basic needs in the industrial era reach saturation. These industries do not necessarily decline, but their growth slows down. New industries emerge that cater to the affluent – consumer-luxury goods, recreation, travel, services, etc.

Technology fundamentally affects both supply and demand. Massive wartime investment in research and development spawns new technology-based industries on the one hand, and brings about obsolescence in others. Internal to the firm, fueled by technological progress, the 'R & D monster' acquires a dynamic of its own, which spawns unasked-for products, increases the technological intensity of the firm and directs the firm's growth thrusts independently and sometimes in spite of the aspirations of the management.

The arrival of affluence casts doubt on economic growth as the main instrument of social progress. Social aspirations shift away from 'quantity' to 'quality' of life. Industrial bigness increasingly appears as a threat, both to economic efficiency through monopolistic practices, and to democracy through 'government-industrial' complexes. Large enterprises are accused of their immoral, 'profiteering', lack of creativity and of failure to enhance efficiency, while increasing in size. Acquisition of other firms is challenged because it is seen to destroy competition. Studies are prepared for dismemberment of giant firms. The growth ethic, which had provided a clear guiding light to social behavior, begins to decline. 'Zero growth' alternatives are advanced, but without a clear understanding of how social vitality is to be retained when growth stops.

Realignment of social priorities focuses attention on the negative side-effects of profit-seeking behavior: environmental pollution, fluctuations in economic activity, inflation, monopolistic practices, 'manipulation' of the consumer through artificial obsolescence, blatant advertising, incomplete disclosure, and low-quality after-sale service. All these effects begin to appear to be too high a price to pay for the laissez-faire conditions of 'free enterprise'. The firm loses its position as the society's 'sacred cow'. But its ability to continue serving society is taken for granted. It is now assumed that the firm is able not only to remain economically efficient under stringent constraints (which only twenty years ago would have been considered fundamentally subversive and socially destructive) but also to undertake 'social responsibility'.

Thus one of the consequences of affluence is the loss of social centrality for the institution that created it. Having 'filled their bellies', individuals begin to aspire to higher levels of personal satisfaction both in their buying and in their working behavior. They become increasingly discriminating – increasingly demanding 'full disclosure' about their purchases, demanding 'post-sales' responsibility from the manufacturer, and unwilling to put up with ecological pollution as a by-product. They begin to lose faith in the wisdom of management and its knowledge of 'what is good for the country'. They challenge the firm directly through 'consumerism' and put pressure on government for increased controls.

Within the firm the traditional solidarity of the managerial class begins to distingrate. Middle managers begin to reject the role of working for the exclusive benefit of the shareholders. The traditional aspiration of every manager to become the president of the firm is not shared by the new generation, which wants the firm to become more socially responsive and to offer opportunities for individual self-fulfillment on the job. Consequently, managers begin to identify with the interests of technocracy rather than with those of the top management or the shareholders.

As another result of affluence, developed nations turn their attention to social problems that remained unsolved while the focus of the nations' energies was on economic growth: social injustice, poverty, housing, education, public transportation, environmental pollution, ecological imbalance. New demands for social services create potential new markets, but, frequently, they cannot be served by profit-seeking behavior.

The firm loses its image as a miraculous 'money-making machine' and is increasingly viewed as a suppressor and impediment to fulfillment of the new social values of clean environment, social equality, secure employment. The U.S. Government, which in the past has confined its regulatory activity to 'preservation of competition', increasingly takes a directive role. For example, it changes the basic technology and product-line strategy of the country's automotive industry. In Western Europe governments come to power which are ideologically hostile to Adam Smith's philosophy. They begin vigorous programs of reshaping the behavior of the firm and diluting the historical power of management.

The private sector is now called upon:

1. to restrain and suppress its socially and physically 'polluting' activities;
2. to provide goods on services in areas where profit cannot be made;
3. to take responsibility for positive social progress.

Thus socio-political transactions with the environment which lay dormant during the earlier eras acquire a life-or-death importance in post-industrial society. They offer opportunities for new commercial activities, impose new social expectations from the firm, and threaten its survival.

At first glance, the turbulence in the post-industrial environment may appear as a return to the days of the industrial revolution. But today's turbulence is much more complex. In the earlier era, creation of marketable products and markets was the major concern of the entrepreneurs. They dreamed grandly and had the genius and energy to convert dreams into reality. But their priorities were almost wholly commercial-entrepreneurial. Having created the business sector, they often lacked the motivation and the capability to settle for the job of competitive exploitation of their creations. Other managers, no less talented, but less visionary and more pragmatic, replaced them and began to elaborate and perfect the production mechanism of the firm and to realize growth and profits. Later, marketeers injected new vitality into the product market environment. Thus the industrial evolution up to the 1950s was a 'sequential' one. It consisted of a succession of periods: entrepreneurial-oriented, production-oriented, marketing-oriented. As one succeeded another, the attention and priorities of management correspondingly shifted from one central preoccupation to another.

But in the 1970s the new priorities do not replace but, rather, add to the previous ones. Competition is not slackening but intensifying as a result of internationalization of business, scarcities of resources, acceleration of technological innovation. Production and distribution problems are growing bigger and more complex. Entrepreneurial concerns with multinational expansion, with technological breakthroughs and obsolescence, with structural changes in the economy, acquire central importance. The firm's relations to government and society emerge as a life-and-death issue. Thus the new concerns come on top of, and not in exchange for, the historical preoccupation with competition and production.

ENVIRONMENT OF THE NON-PROFITS

Through most of this century the environment of the not-for-profits has remained much less turbulent than that of the firm. The firm occupied the center of the societal stage and was the acknowledged leader of social progress. Government, health services, social services, and education were the 'residuals' of the social structure, marginally funded and quiescent. But for this lack of glamor they were rewarded with security. Their continued survival and financial solvency were provided by governmental budgets, endowments and public money raisings. The subsidizing bodies provided a virtually guaranteed income and seldom questioned the responsiveness of the recipient to the needs of his market, nor his internal efficiency in the use of the subsidy. Typically the income from commercial income constituted only a small percentage of the total income of the not-for-profits, and, equally typically, market transactions were conducted at a net loss, which was made up by donations, grants, and subsidies.

As a result entrepreneurial and marketing activity were non-existent in a majority of the non-profit ESOs. They were highly introverted, uncoupled from environmental realities, and internally inefficient.

The roots of change in the United States trace back to the presidency of Franklin D. Roosevelt, who initiated the trend toward 'big government', which increasingly took direct responsibility for social welfare. In developed countries of Western Europe change was triggered, in the post-World War Two period, by new governments committed to the soicalist ideology. As the governments grew, their agencies became increasingly influential on the social scene.

The explosive growth of expenditures for government and social welfare has reached a level at which inefficiency can no longer be tolerated. As a result the not-for-profits are under growing pressure to emulate the efficiency of the business firm. Government ventures into new areas of social need – public health, space exploration, public transportation, preservation of the environment – are forcing non-profits into product-market-creating entrepreneurial activities previously reserved for the firm. The hospital, a recent beneficiary of astronomical growth in health expenditures, faces the prospect of a fundamental shift from curing sick patients to keeping healthy people well. The university, similarly a recent beneficiary of a vast expansion, is confronted with problems of overcapacity, budget deficits and a growing social disenchantment with the irrelevance of the seventeenth-century model of higher education to the problems of the twenty-first century.

Thus in a short space of time the historically quiescent environment of the not-for-profits has become highly turbulent. Because of the speed and the magnitude of the transition, the not-for-profits have an even greater difficulty of adjusting to the new climate than even the most conservative business firms. Bureaucratic ways are so entrenched and resistance to change is so high that it typically takes a near or an actual survival crisis to make an ESO face the new environmental realities. Confronted with this resistance, the government has begun to create new social forms, quasi-commercial, quasi-governmental, which can better serve the new challenges.

To summarize briefly, during the past twenty years a major escalation of environmental turbulence has taken place. For the firm, it has meant a change from the familiar world of marketing and production to an unfamiliar world of strange technologies, strange competitors, new consumer attitudes, new dimensions of social control, and above all, questioning of the firm's role in society. For the non-profits, it has meant a transition from centuries-old introverted perspective to opening of the doors to the environment. The view through the window is on a society which is challenging the social relevance of non-profits on the one hand, and demands expansion of their service and increased effectiveness on the other.

HYPOTHESIS 3.1: CONVERGENCE OF FIRMS AND NON-PROFITS

In the future, the firm's commercial focus will become progressively diluted, and not-for-profits will become more commercial.

MAJOR TRENDS

The preceding discussion shows that during the twentieth century the environment of ESO has progressively increased in turbulence. This can be described by four major trends:

1. Growth of the *novelty* of change. The important events which affect the ESO are progressively disconnected from past experience. We have discussed this phenomenon in detail in the preceding pages;

2. Growth in the *intensity* of the environment. The maintenance of linkages between the ESO and its correspondents
consumes a growing percentage of energy, resources, and
managerial attention. We shall devote the following chapter
to analysis of strategic intensity;
3. Increase in the *speed* of environmental change;
4. Growing *complexity* of the environment.

We deal with the last two factors in the following paragraphs.

In the past thirty years, numerous studies have been made of
the acceleration of environmental change. An important common
conclusions of these studies is that the time between emergence
and commercialization of new technology is progressively shrinking. We illustrate this phenomenon in Figure 3.1, where the graph
shows a progressive and dramatic shrinkage in commercialization
time of succeeding key technologies.

A companion aspect of speed is the rate of diffusion of
commercialized change among the users. This is illustrated in

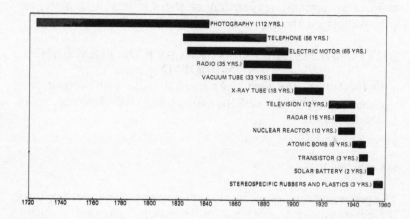

Figure 3.1   Speed of Commercialization Change

*Source: Center for Integrative Studies, World Facts and Trends (Binghamton,
New York: School of Advanced Technology, State University of New York,
1969).*

Figure 3.2 where the curve labelled 'speed of technological change' represents a reciprocal of the commercialization times of Figure 3.1. The other curves show the rapidity of diffusion of products during the second half of the twentieth century.

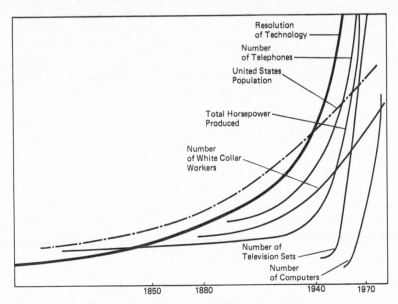

Figure 3.2 Speed of Diffusion of Change

Together the two curves show that over the past hundred years there has been a dramatic shrinkage of the time lag between invention and full market penetration. They also suggest that the rate of invention has been accelerating.

In addition to speed of change, there has also been a marked increase in the complexity of the environment. We have illustrated this by gathering from the preceding discussion a comparison of the salient characteristics of the industrial and the post-industrial environments. This comparison is shown in Figure 3.3.

As the upper part of the figure shows, the boundaries of the traditional industries are expanding, while becoming more permeable and more difficult to define. The commercial and the socio-political worlds are becoming increasingly interconnected. As a result, industrial activity is influenced by an increasing number of actors and many of the important influences on the

Figure 3.3   Complexity of the Environment

Attribute	Period Industrial (1900–1950s)	Post-Industrial (1950s–)
Boundary of environment	Around commercial activity of the ESO	Includes commercial socio-political activity
	Stable	Changing
	Well-defined	Vague
	Non-permeable	Permeable to new influences
	Few different types of actors	Many different types of actors
	Environment segmentated into industries	Industry lines indistinct
	Influences among actors largely direct	Direct and indirect influences
	Firm the center of power	Centers of power in political bodies
	Common shared knowledge	Many foci of privileged knowledge
Dynamics of environment	Environmental change generated by the ESO	Change generated both inside ESO and outside environment by many sources
	Few surprises	Many surprises
	Technology, markets, continuously evolving	Discontinuous changes frequent in market structure, technology, government relations.
	Occasional discontinuities	
	Prior experience applicable to new situations	Prior experience inapplicable to new situations

ESO are indirect, brought to bear through intermediate partners. (Example: the indirect but persuasive and fundamental influence exercised on all industries by the Arab countries since they took over control of petroleum production and pricing).

The lower part shows some key consequences for the environmental dynamics. ESOs, particularly the firm, have lost their position as the sole originators of change in their industries. Change now comes from many quarters, and because it is frequently indirect and comes from outside the industry, it is increasingly surprising and novel. Historical experience is decreasingly applicable.

The figure suggests that the advent of the post-industrial era represents a genuine increase in the level of turbulence. The figure also suggests that events in the environment are becoming less predictable in two ways: (1) For actions originating with an ESO it is increasingly difficult to predict their full consequences. This results partly from the far-reaching impact of the actions, and partly from unexpected reactions and counteractions by the many affected correspondents. (2) For actions originated by others it is increasingly difficult to anticipate the source and the nature of the actions, because of the multiplicity, unfamiliarity and remoteness of the sources.

HYPOTHESIS 3.2: GROWTH OF ENVIRONMENTAL TURBULENCE

During the twentieth century the key events in the environment of ESOs have become progressively: (1) novel; (2) costlier to deal with; (3) faster; (4) more difficult to anticipate.

4 Model of Budgeting Behavior

'The rule is, jam tomorrow and jam yesterday – but never jam today.' 'It *must* come sometimes to "jam today",' Alice objected. 'No, it can't,' said the Queen. 'It's jam every other day: today isn't any *other* day, you know.'

Lewis Carroll

The most visible and most prevalent decision-making activity in the ESO is the process of resource allocation. In this chapter we discuss budgeting as a key form of strategic behavior by the ESO.

STRATEGIC INTENSITY

An ESO is usually a member of a group of similar organizations which have the following common features. All of the members:

1. Sell similar products/services to a common pool of customers/clients;
2. Buy their inputs from a common group of suppliers;
3. Obtain their subsidies from a common pool of donors;
4. Share a common body of knowhow, called *technology*, which is essential for their commercial activity.

In business such a set of interrelated groups, composed of ESOs, customers, suppliers, and financing sources is called an *industry*. This term is increasingly applied to not-for-profit groupings such as the 'hospital industry', 'the higher education industry', etc.

From the viewpoint of each group of participants, an important characteristic of their industry is what we call its *intensity* –

the amount of energy members of the group devote to interaction with others. In a given industry each group of actors perceives the intensity according to its own involvement. Thus intensity is not a general, but an actor-specific measure. Since our interest is focused on ESOs, we shall use their view of intensity to characterize the industry. This intensity can be conveniently measured by the budgets ESOs devote to strategic action.

Definition: The *strategic intensity* of an industry can be measured by the strategic budgets of the participant ESOs.

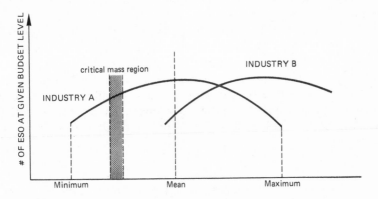

Figure 4.1   Distribution of Strategic Budgets in Two Industries

Figure 4.1 illustrates two distributions of strategic budgets. Industry A clearly has the higher intensity, both its average and maximum budgets are higher than those of industry B.

The total strategic budgets shown in Figure 4.1 consist of two parts: (1) The *marketing budget* which supports sales of the ESO products and purchases of the necessary resources, and (2) the *entrepreneurial budget* which supports innovative activities, such as changing the character of the products, markets, technology and basic sources of supply. Each budget serves a different but complementary strategic need of an ESO. Marketing assures sales of the current products to the current customers, while entrepreneurship changes both the products and the markets. Overemphasis on marketing of products which have become obsolete will lead to a decline in income, but so will changes in the products before marketing has a chance to exploit them fully. Marketing activity produces near-term results for the ESO, whereas the entrepreneurial activity creates a long-term potential, while depressing results in the near term. Thus both survival and success of an ESO depend on a judicious allocation of the strategic budget between the marketing and the entrepreneurial activities.

In microeconomic literature high marketing budgets are taken as a sign of vigorous competitive activity; and competitive vigor is related to the industrial concentration. Strong competition is predicted for multi-competitor industries in which no firm holds a commanding share, weak competition for monopolistic industries.

But competitive structure alone does not explain either the competitive vigor or large marketing budgets. There are industries with widely distributed shares in which competition is weak, and there are monopolies (e.g. The Bell Telephone Corporation) with large marketing budgets, which continuously seek to improve services to their customers. Thus other variables are needed to explain the degree of an ESOs involvement in marketing.

The key variables are:

1. The ratio of the total market demand in the industry to the total available industrial capacity. A low ratio will stimulate marketing activity regardless of the industry's structure;
2. The marketing aggressiveness of the leading competitors in the industry. Industries have been shocked out of their competitive doldrums by entry of new competitors (e.g. entry of Japanese steel in the U.S. market);
3. The legislative restrictions which enforce certain types of marketing behavior. These may reduce the cost of marketing (through prohibiting certain competitive practices), or increase it (e.g. legislation requiring 'truth in advertising');
4. Customer pressures and 'buyer's resistance' brought to bear on an ESO. Strong resistance will enhance marketing budgets, even if competition is weak.

Thus for studying the marketing intensity of an industry, it is useful to enlarge the concept of competition to a concept of environmental resistance:

Definition: Environmental resistance is the sum total of the pressures by the other actors in the industry, as well as from the outside forces, which increases the budget needed by an ESO to sell its output to the customers.

It follows, by definition, that the marketing budgets in an industry are correlated to the environmental resistance within it.

A similar concept is useful for identifying the pressures on the entrepreneurial budgets. The pressures for higher budgets can come from:

1. The rate of technological innovation caused by the fertility of the industry's technology, or by invasion of the industry by a new technology;
2. Saturation of demand for the products currently offered in the industry;
3. Entrepreneurially aggressive competition by leaders of the industry;
4. Legislation (e.g. automotive safety, anti-pollution);
5. Customer demand for innovation.

Definition: *Innovation pressure* is the sum total of the pressures in an industry which increase the budgets needed by an ESO to make its products saleable to the customers.

(It will be convenient for future discussion to refer to the sum of the environmental resistance and of the innovation pressures as the *environmental impedance*.)

HYPOTHESIS 4.1: STRATEGIC INTENSITY AND ENVIRONMENTAL IMPEDANCE

The level of marketing budgets in an industry is correlated to its environmental resistance, while the level of the entrepreneurial budget is correlated to its innovation pressure.

ENVIRONMENTAL DEPENDENCE

Environmental impedance is helpful for explaining differences in strategic budget level among business firms. But it is not sufficient to explain the distinctive behavior of non-profits in which strategic budgets are typically non-existent, in spite of the fact that some of them are subject to much customer dissatisfaction and legislative prodding.

We suggest that the key explanatory factor of the difference lies in the respective dependence of firms and non-profits on their commercial activity.

The privately owned business firm is totally dependent on the market. The financial support received from the subsidy environment increases this dependence. Business subsidies come in two forms: equity invested in the firm by shareholders and loans provided by public agencies and financial institutions. Both impose repayment obligations. Equity investment requires dividends, loans a fixed rate of interest. Under most conditions these subsidies may be used only for expansion and diversification of the firm and may not be used for making up operating deficits. If the firm incurs a deficit, equity investors will leave, its access to further borrowing funds will be blocked, and current lending agents will impose restrictions and will seek to control the behavior of the firm.

By contrast, not-for-profit ESOs typically derive only a minor portion of their current income from commercial transactions. These are typically conducted at a loss and operating deficits are made up by subsidies from government agencies, individual philanthropists, and philanthropic foundations. The reason for this behavior is that, unlike the firm, the size and availability of subsidies is independent of the ESOs commercial effectiveness. The size of grants is determined by legal obligations, societal need for the service provided by the ESO, personal generosity of individuals. The duration of the grants is based on continuance of the societal need, personal loyalties, the 'giving habit', nostalgia for the alma mater, etc.

Thus to assure survival and success, the firm is driven into strategic action which makes its commercial activity profitable and effective. A highly subsidized non-profit is virtually discouraged from strategic activity. We have demonstrated the perspective patterns of influence on the two institutions in Figure 4.2.

The patterns suggest that there are two complementary ways to induce non-profits to engage in more vigorous strategic behavior: (1) to increase their dependence on the commercial income, and (2) to make the availability of subsidy dependent on the commercial performance. Neither of these conditions has been

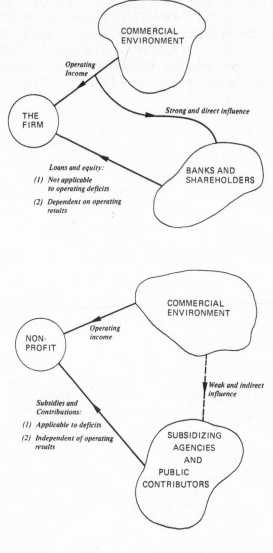

Figure 4.2   Differences in Market Dependence

enforced in recent social experiments (e.g. the U.S. Post Office), which sought to convert not-for-profits into for-profits. As a result, the for-profit status became a pro-forma window dressing, and the dynamics of the ESOs behavior remained unchanged.

HYPOTHESIS 4.2: EFFECT OF ENVIRONMENTAL DEPENDENCE ON STRATEGIC BUDGETS

The budgets allocated by an ESO to its strategic activity are correlated to the fraction of its total income obtained from the commercial environment, and to the degree of dependence of the subsidy income on the level of the ESOs strategic activity.

CRITICAL MASS

We now return to Figure 4.1 and the lower budget range to analyze the borderline between survival and non-survival in an industry. At the lower budget end ESOs are usually feeble, unprofitable performers, which are either in the process of being squeezed out of the industry, or require large subsidies to stay alive. Between these failure-prone ESOs and the successful ones is a narrow band of budget levels, labelled 'critical mass' in Figure 4.1.

Definition: *Critical mass* is the budget level just adequate to enable an ESO to continue to recover its costs from the commercial environment.

The critical mass is a concept widely discussed in business literature, but poorly complied with in practice. Failures to pay attention to the critical mass level can have dramatic consequences, particularly in new industries based on revolutionary technologies. A recent example occured in the 'mainframe' computer industry, where giant firms such as General Electric, RCA, and Philips made both an enthusiastic early entry and a later disillusioned exit. To a large extent the exit was forced by a belated recognition that the critical mass was higher than the respective firms could afford to put into competing with the dominant IBM.

Two component measures determine the critical mass. The first, particularly important in emerging industries, is the minimum start-up investment in product-market development facilities, inventories and skills which is necessary to establish a viable foothold in the industry. In firms, the size of this foothold is often measured by the critical market share. The second component is the annual budget that the ESO needs to commit in order to maintain the critical market share. We shall refer to the two components as the *start-up* and the *sustaining* critical mass respectively.

The total start-up critical mass is an entrepreneurial expense and belongs entirely to the strategic budget. The sustaining critical mass is in three parts. The first is an *entrepreneurial critical mass* which is the minimum expense needed for keeping the ESOs offerings up to date. The size of the entrepreneurial critical mass is correlated with the innovation pressure in the environment.

The second part is the *marketing critical mass*, correlated to the environmental resistance, which is the minimum budget needed to assure sales of the ESO output, sufficient for a break-even operation. The third is the *operating critical mass* needed to keep the production costs low enough to make the output saleable at a break-even. The operating critical mass is high in industries in which the output is mass-produced and investment in production technology is high; it is low in industries with 'hand-made' output and low technology.

Thus the total critical mass of an ESO is the sum of the respective parts

$$m_{cr} = m_{cr}^e + m_{cr}^m + m_c^o$$

At critical mass, an ESO is barely able to break even in the industry. As the budget begins to exceed the critical mass, the ESO gains in stature and influence. It is able to offer up-to-date products and gain further economies of scale from its marketing and operations. Thus its economic effectivenessness rises. But beyond a certain point the marginal increases in effectiveness will begin to decrease. What is gained through greater market penetration begins to be lost through loss in efficiency caused by size, complexity, loss of flexibility.

We therefore hypothesize that the effectiveness of an ESOs budget will eventually level off, after the budget reaches a certain level. In future discussions we will represent the effectiveness of the budget by the relation

$$E = f\left(\frac{B}{m_{cr}}\right)$$

where E is the effectiveness and B is the budget. The function E is such that

$$E < 0 \text{ for } B < m_{cr}$$
$$E \text{ increases in the range } M_{cr} < B \leq \overline{B}$$
$$E = \overline{E} \text{ for all values of } B \text{ above } \overline{B}.$$

We summarize this section through the following hypotheses:

HYPOTHESIS 4.3: CRITICAL MASS
In for-profit industries there are minimal entrepreneurial, marketing and operating budgets which an ESO must commit to the industry in order to remain viable.

HYPOTHESIS 4.4: CRITICAL SIZE
When the total critical mass in an industry is larger than the total budget available to an ESO, the ESO is too small to participate profitably in the industry.

BUDGET MIX

Since, for viability, each budget component must be at or above its own critical mass level, misallocation of budgets in an ESO can have serious consequences. An ESO whose total budget is above m_{cr} but which underbudgets one of the components will suffer losses. It must eventually either raise the subcritical budget or withdraw from the industry.

We can examine the consequences of different budget allocations with the help of Figure 4.3, which shows different possible budgets as percentages of the total budget of an ESO. The line connecting the two 100 per cent points encloses a triangle of all possible budget allocations. The allocations which fall on this line divide the budget between marketing and entrepreneurship and leave nothing for operations, which is clearly a nonviable way of partitioning the total strategic budget (unless the ESO is non-producing middleman, or its product *is* R & D). Viable budget combinations are represented for each activity by the shaded triangle whose boundaries are the critical masses for each activity. These boundaries are obtained by dividing the respective critical masses for the industry by the total budget of the ESO and by

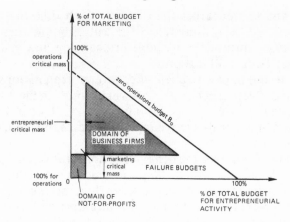

Figure 4.3 Budgeting and Critical Mass

drawing the respective lines, as shown in the figure. The result will be as shown if each of the three critical masses is smaller than the total budget. If at least one of the critical masses exceeds the total available, the triangle will collapse, which means that the ESO is too small to be viable in the particular industry.

Within the domain of viable budgets there is an area which will produce the best economic results. The location of this area depends on the relative importance of the three primary activities to the success on the market place. It will be recalled that during the industrial revolution entrepreneurial activity was dominant. Hence the budgets of the most successful firms were to be found in the right-hand corner of the triangle. During the mass-production era the optimal region shifted to the lower left-hand corner where the operating budget is the largest. During the mass-marketing period the optimal region shifted toward the upper-left hand corner. The post-industrial turbulence is shifting the success region toward the center of the triangle, which implies a need for simultaneous managerial concern with all three activities.

During the respective periods there were 'success regions' in the respective parts of the triangle which were occupied by a small percentage of the best performers in the industry. The remainder formed a scatter pattern around the optimum, some emphasizing operations, some marketing, and some entrepreneurship.

When the optimal region shifted, some firms quickly adjusted their budgeting mix, but a majority typically lagged behind, making the scatter larger than before. With time the majority moved toward the optimum and the scatter boundaries shrank. Thus whether turbulence is stable or changing, few firms maximize their budget allocations.

Later in the book, we shall offer several explanations for the scatter of budgeting behavior. One will be found in the differences in performance aspirations among ESOs; another in imperfect perception of where the budgeting region lies; a third in difference in 'work cultures'.

As Figure 4.3 shows, the behavior of non-profits is usually in or near the shaded left-hand rectangle in which most of the budget is comitted to operations. As discussed earlier, this is due to the fact that not-for-profits usually have no incentive to invest in their marketing and their products. But as we shall discuss later, many non-profit industries are inherently non-profitable so that no amount of marketing and entrepreneurship can make them commercially viable. In the terminology of Fig 4.3 this means that in such industries both the marketing and the entrepreneurial masses are larger than any total budget an ESO may have. In this case the two vertical lines intersect outside the 100 per cent line and there is no viable region.

HYPOTHESIS 4.5: OPTIMAL BUDGETING
In each industry at a given point in time there is a region of budget mixes which will produce optimal economic results.

HYPOTHESIS 4.6: ESO BUDGETING BEHAVIOR
Most ESOs do not budget optimally. During periods of transition of the optimal budget region, ESOs typically lag in adjusting their budget mixes.

5 Model of Environmental Turbulence

'If we could first know where we are and whither we are tending, we could better judge what to do and how to do it.'

Abraham Lincoln

At the end of Chapter 3, we identified four major factors which have contributed to the growing turbulence of the environment. In the preceding chapter we modelled one of these: the strategic budgeting. In this chapter we shall first model the remaining three factors: novelty, speed and predictability. Second, we shall integrate these factors into a scale of environmental turbulence. Third, we shall show how the scale of turbulence can be used to predict the success of an ESOs strategic behavior.

PREDICTABILITY

Each change in the environment goes through a natural evolution which progressively increases the available knowledge. At the earliest stage, it is possible only to identify a general state of turbulence in the environment, a rumbling before the earthquake. For example, in the electronics industry in the early 1940s there was a general sense of expectation of important breakthroughs and developments. The electronics industry was the one to watch and to invest in. In the early postwar years, it became increasingly clear to the experts that a likely source of breakthrough would be the new phenomenon of semiconduction. It was not, however, until the actual invention of the transistor in 1946 that the nature of the breakthrough became concrete: a specific new operating device had appeared called the transistor. As the operating and physical characteristics of the transistor became better understood, it became increasingly possible to assess its potential impact on the industry. Later, the affected and interested firms began to define specific actions, either for entry into the transistor business, or for counteracting the impact of the transistors.

At this stage the full profit consequences of the various responses still remained unclear. But some entrepreneurial and forward-looking firms committed themselves to action in the expectation that 'an early bird gets the worm'. The profit consequences become increasingly clear as crystal growing, slicing, and impurity implantation technologies were reduced to mass-production. But the estimates of the consequences were still subject to uncertainty since they were based on conjecture and not performance. Then the transistor was launched commercially and the first concrete results began to come in. As these results cumulated, the final step in the development of knowledge arrived when the full impact of the transistor was realized. For some firms this meant an established market position and clear prospects of future growth; to others it meant a permanent loss of profits.

In Figure 5.1 we have generalized the transistor example into a typical sequence of increasing knowledge (or decreasing ignorance) states associated with all changes in the environment. Labelled across the top are seven levels of successively increasing knowledge. The left-hand column describes the steps in the progression of knowledge. The 'Yes' and 'No' entries show how new knowledge cumulates with time.

Readers familiar with mathematical decision theory will recognize Figure 5.1 as an extension of that theory. The figure makes explicit a dimension usually left implicit, namely, the *information content* of the alternatives under consideration. The decision theory assumes that the information content is in state (5) and concerns itself with the uncertainties in the occurrence and outcomes of fully specified events. Our extension makes operational the concept of *partial ignorance* which was first introduced in my book *Corporate Strategy* in 1965.

While all new phenomena develop through the successive states of knowledge shown in Figure 5.1, the speed of evolution differs. A useful measure of the speed is the time which remains until full impact at each succeeding state of knowledge. We demonstrate this graphically in Figure 5.2. The dotted line *A* at the top is a change which repeats other identical changes which have occurred in the past. For example, this may be a recurrence of a short-

Information Content	(1) Sense of Turbulence	(2) Source Identified	(3) Impact Identified	(4) Response Determined	(5) Outcome Estimated	(6) First Impact	(7) Full impact
Conviction that discontinuities are pending	YES	YES	YES	YES	YES	YES	YES
The technology, the source of market disturbance or socio-political change identified	NO	YES	YES	YES	YES	YES	YES
Characteristics, nature, gravity, and timing of impact can be estimated, subject to uncertainty of occurrence	NO	NO	YES	YES	YES	YES	YES
Response identified: timing, action, programs, budgets can be identified	NO	NO	NO	YES	YES	YES	YES
Outcome of response is computable, subject to uncertainty	NO	NO	NO	NO	YES	YES	YES
First impact of change is felt through operating results	NO	NO	NO	NO	NO	YES	YES
Full impact of change is felt	NO	NO	NO	NO	NO	NO	YES

Figure 5.1 Evolution of Knowledge About an Environmental Change

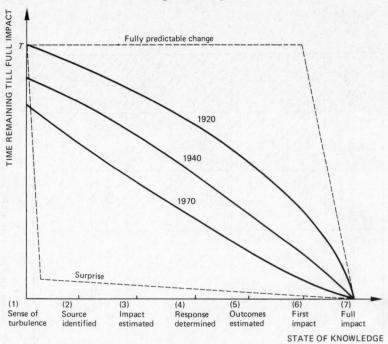

Figure 5.2   Predictability of Change

lived 'price war', through discounts on gasoline prices, which has been a regular feature in the petroleum industry. It is instantly recognizable the minute it occurs. Therefore, we represent it by a horizontal line until the actual impact begins.

The lower dotted line *B* is the other extreme of a change which has not occurred before. It is born 'full blown' without prior warning. It will be a surprise to the affected ESO, regardless of the efforts they make to predict it.

The two dotted curves form an envelope of possible change histories which are first signalled by a general sense of turbulence at time *T* ahead of their full impact. Using solid curves, we have demonstrated between the extremes the evolution of the change patterns during the twentieth century. Each line represents a typical history of change at the succeeding points in time.

The progressive decrease of time *T* at which signs of change first become evident is related to the phenomenon of complexity which we discussed in Chapter 3. As the important changes increasingly originate from sources outside the historical industry boundaries, it becomes increasingly difficult to recognize the change and its implications. This was certainly the case in the 'petroleum crisis'; this now is the case in the impending limitations on industrial growth.

The change of curvature of the respective curves from the slow drop of the 1920s to the fast curve of the 1970s reflects our previous discussion of the acceleration of the rate of propagation of change from its inception to its full impact on the environment. To use a military analogy, Figure 5.2 shows that the range of the radars for early recognition of potential attackers is shrinking and the speed with which the attackers fly is increasing. As the graph shows, change has become progressively faster, while the time T has been shrinking due to complexity, interconnectedness of the environment, and increasingly foreign origins.

Definition: Given two change histories, we shall call the change that leaves more time impact at all states of information the more *inherently predictable* of the two.

HYPOTHESIS 5.1: DECREASING PREDICTABILITY
During the twentieth century, the predictability of environmental change has been progressively decreasing.

NOVELTY OF CHANGE

Whether predictability is important, depends on the magnitude of the impact and the time needed by the affected ESO to respond to the change. If the impact is minor, and response is rapid, predictability does not matter. The ESO can react after the full impact has been felt. This is a frequent case in both firms and non-profits in dealing with numerous changes whose 'full impact' does not amount to very much.

But advance notice which permits time for preparation and action may be important when the impact of the change is consequential. The importance will depend on how much time an ESO needs for an effective response, and this time depends on the novelty of the change.

Definition: The novelty of a change is a measure of the *inapplicability* of the ESOs capability to deal with the change.

If a change is a repetition of past changes, most ESOs will have a built-up capability for handling it. For an effective response such ESOs will need only enough time to execute previously developed response programs. If, on the other hand, the change is totally novel, none of the prior capabilities will apply and substantial additional time is needed to gather the necessary resources and to train people, to build facilities, and to develop and test new programs. The execution of the new programs will be a first-time experience and will take longer than comparable familiar well-exercised programs.

Thus we can subdivide the total response time needed by an ESO into two parts: the capability build-up time and the execution time:

$$T_R = T_c + T_e$$

For fully familiar changes $T_c^f = 0$; for totally new changes the preparation time is usually longer than the execution $T_c^n > T_e^n$, as well as $T_e^n > T_e^f$.

In Figure 5.3 we have demonstrated the curves of the response times as a function of the state of knowledge at which a firm starts its response. The two solid curves demonstrate the extremes: the lower is response to the totally familiar change, and the upper to a change to which no part of the existing capability is applicable. In between the two curves we have illustrated the progression of the response curve during the twentieth century. As discussed, a major reason for the upward displacement of the curves is the increasing inapplicability of prior capabilities. But another reason, not directly visible in the figure, has been the growth in size and complexity of ESOs. In large and complex ESOs the inherent time delays have been increasing in parallel with novelty, thus compounding the increase in the time required for both capability development and program execution.

As the curvature of the graphs shows, an ESO needs more time if it chooses to respond at early states of knowledge, than it needs for a late start. In the latter case, all the necessary information is available and the various components of response can be planned and executed in an efficient sequence. If the response is started early, the actions which can be taken will be limited by the

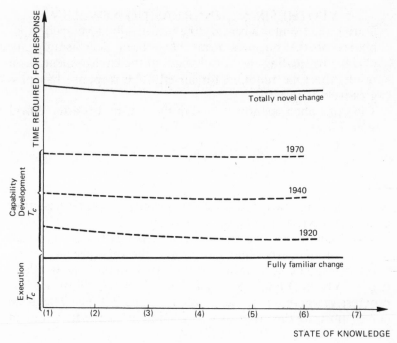

Figure 5.3 Response Time vs Novelty vs Early Start of Response

available information. Thus, for example, if the firm starts its response in state (1), all it can do is intensify its general environmental surveillance. As additional knowledge becomes available, additional partial response steps become possible. Such environment-determined sequence of responses is likely to be less efficient than a well-planned response started under complete information about impending change.

Thus, other things being equal, an ESO is well advised to apply what President Eisenhower once called the 'delay principle' – to delay the response until all of the essential information becomes available. But, as we have already shown in the preceding section, other things are not equal. The response must be squeezed into the time available before the impact of change, and, under decreasing predictability, the time available under the delay principle is likely to be insufficient. Thus, ESOs are being forced to start their response at progressively earlier states of knowledge. We shall illustrate this graphically in the following section.

HYPOTHESIS 5.2: INCREASING NOVELTY

During the twentieth century the historically developed capabilities of the business firms have been decreasingly applicable to treating the key changes in the environment. As a result, the time required for an effective response has progressively increased.

The same phenomenon started in the non-profits after World War Two.

ESCALATION OF TURBULENCE

As the preceding two sections show, during the twentieth century business firms (and during the second half of the century the non-profits) found themselves in an uncomfortable situation in which the time available became shorter and the time needed for an effective response became longer. We have brought together these two trends in Figure 5.4. The dotted curves illustrate the progressive increase in the needed response time. The solid curves illustrate the progressive reduction in the predictability of events.

The intersections of the contemporaneous pairs of curves at points *A*, *B* and *C* represent critical crossover points: if an ESO starts its response to the right of the point, the time made available by the change will not be sufficient for an effective response. As the figure shows, the historical trend displaced the crossover point to progressively earlier states of knowledge.

As point *A* drifted toward *B*, firms were under pressure to react at an earlier state of knowledge. Their initial reaction was to shorten the response time through rapid processing of information about results and through expeditious use of this information. *Management reporting* systems based on accounting data were developed to accomplish the first purpose, and *management control* systems for the second.

But as the crossover moved in the region between states of knowledge (5) and (6), historical accounting for results after impact became inadequate. Response had to be started before the impact. Firms responded to this pressure by inventing *extrapolative forecasting* for acquiring the environmental information and *long-range* planning for using it. The former was able to capture information about change while it was still between states

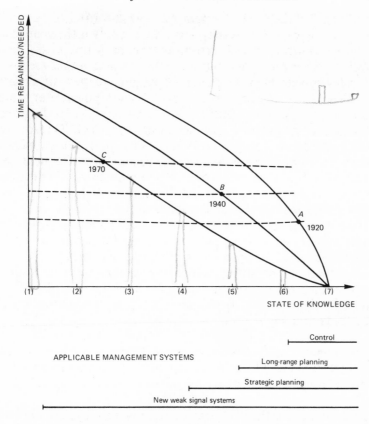

*Figure 5.4   Shifting Relation Between Predictability
and Novelty*

(5) and (6), and the latter introduced decision-making based on
conjectures about the future, rather than on past results.

As the crossover point moved into the region between states (4)
and (5), extrapolative forecasting and the accompanying decision
methods used in long-range planning became inadequate, because they work only when outcomes of responses are specifiable.
Again, firms reacted by inventing new *non-extrapolative forecasting* techniques (called 'Threat/opportunity analysis' in business
planning literature) which work in the region between states (4)
and (5). To use the new, less complete information, *strategic
planning* was invented.

As Figure 5.4 suggests, growing environmental turbulence has already shifted the crossover point beyond state (4). For many of today's changes, timely response is possible only if the change is perceived before concrete responses can be formulated. New decision and response techniques, such as *issue analysis*, are now being developed which permit firms to respond to the *weak signals* provided by a change in early states of its development. For some changes the crossover point has already moved beyond the sense of turbulence point (state 1), which means that the ESO response to such changes will be inevitably late. This type of situation is an *inherent strategic surprise*. As surprises become more frequent, we predict that, following tradition or adaptation, firms will develop *surprise management* systems. At the bottom of Figure 5.4, we have summarized the range of applicability of different systems.

If we examine the nature of the shifts of the respective crossover points, it becomes clear that at the different states of novelty the methods required for abstracting information from the environment, as well as capabilities required for handling the information are not continuous but discrete. It is useful, therefore, to introduce the concept of *turbulence levels* in the environment. This leads to a key definition.

Definition: *The level of turbulence* in an industry is the state of knowledge at which ESOs in the industry must start response in order to respond effectively to environmental changes.

In the course of the evolution of an industry there are natural turbulence transition points. At birth new industries are highly turbulent with many technologies and many competitors striving to gain dominance over each other. Novelty is high, predictability is low and crossover point lies between states (1) and (2). In the second phase turbulence drops substantially as the industry, 'rationalized' from its early turbulent days, embarks on a period of rapid and sustained growth. The crossover point is now around states (6) and (7), the environment is highly predictable and change is repetitive. The next shift occurs when growth can no longer be sustained by unfilled demand and various stimulants come into use. Finally, when stimulation no longer works, the industry settles into a slow growth or stagnation and eventual decline.

In the course of the natural evolution, turbulence may be enhanced by singular events which upset the natural pattern. The process may be gradual, such as the current process of re-distribution of power within the firm; or the change in turbulence may be rapid and surprising, such as the invention of the transistor.

During the first half of the twentieth century, many of the key industries born in the nineteenth century went through the second and third stages of the natural evolution without major disruptions.

In the second half of the century, many of the first-generation industries if left to themselves would have moved to slowdown and some to saturation of growth. But opening of global markets, invasion by foreign technology, impact of the body politic acted to enhance turbulence. The general turbulence of the environment was further enhanced by 'second-generation' industries born of new technologies and new societal affluence. In the early 1970s the crossover point in many industries has moved to states (2) and (3).

HYPOTHESIS 5.3: ESCALATION OF TURBULENCE
During the twentieth century the level of turbulence has progressively escalated in most industries.

EVOLUTION OF ORGANIZATIONAL INTELLIGENCE

The preceding discussion illustrates behavior which can be called learning behavior. Under pressure of adverse experience, firms have progressively learned to adapt their response mechanisms to the increasing turbulence of the environment. But not all firms were alike. Some were early pioneers of the new techniques; others willing and even avid adopters of the new inventions; still others resisted learning until it became necessary for survival. Thus we can say that, in a given industry at a given time, we would expect to find substantial differences in the *intelligence* of firms.

As already mentioned, organizational learning among non-profit ESOs was very much slower during the first part of the century, primarily because their environments were quiescent: predictability was high and stable, and novelty was low. But after the 1950s, as the environment began to 'heat up', non-profits gradually began to adapt the technologies developed in business firms.

The historical evolution of intelligence enabled ESOs to deal with increasing discontinuities from past experience. Most of this evolution was *reactive* in response to unsatisfactory performance caused by escalation of turbulence. In recent years, however, there have increasingly appeared instances of *anticipatory* learning, in which firms seek to develop ways for dealing with new aspects of turbulence before they produce a serious impact on the firm. One explanation which can be offered for this behavior is that firms are increasingly becoming aware of the importance of adjusting their capabilities to the changing turbulence. Another is that turbulence is growing so rapidly that after-the-fact learning cannot keep up with the change.

HYPOTHESIS 5.4: ORGANIZATIONAL LEARNING
ESOs respond to drops in predictability and increase in novelty by developing appropriate response capabilities.

HYPOTHESIS 5.5: EVOLUTION OF ORGANIZATIONAL INTELLIGENCE
1. Throughout the twentieth century firms have progressively developed capabilities for dealing with changes which are discontinuous from past experience.
2. During the second half of the twentieth century firms increasingly began to anticipate the need for new response capabilities.

SCALE OF TURBULENCE

The average trends in the escalation of turbulence, while descriptive of the environment as a whole, are not adequate for analysis of strategic behavior. As already indicated, different industries within the average pattern find themselves on different levels. Thus, for example, in today's generally turbulent environment the computer industry is clearly in a more turbulent state than basic chemicals, and the health industry more turbulent than the education industry.

For purposes of illustration we propose to construct a graphic model of turbulence. We borrow an analogy from the early orbital concept of the atom in which electrons change their location in discrete orbits whenever an appropriate impulse occurs.

The analogy is based on our previous observation that the four factors which contribute to environmental turbulence move together. These four factors are: (1) Strategic budget level; (2) Unpredictability of change; (3) Novelty of change; (4) Frequency of change.

The graphic analogy of the orbital concept, shown in Figure 5.5, accommodates the following features:

1. The orbits represent distinctive states of turbulence;
2. The radius of the orbit represents the strategic budget;
3. The frequency of the oscillations in each orbit is the frequency of change on a given level of turbulence;
4. The amplitude of the oscillations is a measure of the novelty of change in the respective orbits.

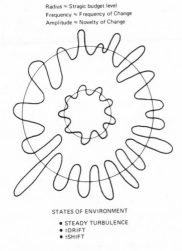

Radius ≈ Stragic budget level
Frequency ≈ Frequency of Change
Amplitude ≈ Novelty of Change

STATES OF ENVIRONMENT
● STEADY TURBULENCE
● ±DRIFT
● ±SHIFT

Figure 5.5   Orbital analogy of Turbulence

Definition: In further discussions we shall confine ourselves to the following states of the environment:

1. *Steady turbulence*, in which the environment remains in a particular orbit;
2. *Shift* in turbulence, which is a rapid transition from one orbit to another;

3. *Drift* in turbulence, which is a gradual transition from one orbit to another.

In the remainder of this book, we shall also confine our attention to five distinctive levels of environmental turbulence which are intended to span the range which may be found in an industry. For easy reference we give a name to each of the levels, which is intended to evoke an image of the respective turbulence levels. These names are listed across the top of Figure 5.6. At one extreme is the *stable*, completely quiescent environment; at the other is a *creative* environment, characterized by major technological breakthroughs, or socio-political upheavals.

In the left-hand column of Figure 5.6, we have gathered the attributes which contribute to determining a turbulence level. The *strategic budget* intensity is defined as the percentage of the total budgets of the ESO in an industry that is spent on strategic activity. (In business firms a frequently used, and imperfect, measure is the percentage of sales spent on R & D.)

The range of *predictability* varies in accordance with the earlier Figure 5.2. The *response time* is a measure which is relative to an industry's history but also depends on the size, complexity and technological intensity of the ESO within a given industry. Response times in a highly technologically intensive oligopoly may be high for all levels of turbulence when compared to simpler, less concentrated industries. As seen from the figure, the discreteness of the respective states of turbulence is introduced by the last three attributes.

The use of the multiple attributes permits an assessment of turbulence on several colinear criteria, thus offering a weight of evidence. The colinearity of attributes is not meant to imply that, in any given industry, the values of all the attributes will fall in a single column. Typically the result is a profile which zig-zags but seldom spans more than two columns. A mean vertical line through the profile can be used to define the state of turbulence in the industry.

The turbulence scale of Figure 5.5 can be used to characterize commercial, political, or subsidy environments. But the generality of the attributes makes them difficult to measure.

For practical applications, we have developed more concrete turbulence scales for the commercial environment. It will be recalled from our discussion of history that the turbulence levels

CHARACTERISTICS OF CHANGE	STABLE	REACTIVE	ANTICIPATORY	EXPLORING	CREATIVE
STRATEGIC BUDGET INTENSITY (% of total budget)	LOW				HIGH
PREDICTABILITY	Most changes fully predictable				Frequent surprises
FREQUENCY	LOW				HIGH
RESPONSE TIME	SHORT				LONG
NOVELTY (applicability of historical capability)	Capability applies	Incremental adjustment	Incremental expansion	Novel combination of existing capabilities	Novel capabilities needed
TURBULENCE LEVEL (State of knowledge for successful response)	Full Impact (7)	First Impact (6)	Outcome estimated (5)	Response determined or impact determined (4) or (3)	Source identified or sense of turbulence (2) or (1)
APPLICABLE FORECASTING TECHNOLOGY	Use of precedents	Management control	Extrapolation	Threat/opport. analysis or weak signal detection	Weak signal detection

Figure 5.6 Scale of Environmental Turbulence in an industry

Figure 5.7 Levels of Entrepreneurial Turbulence

Level of Turbulence Attributes	Stable (1)	Reactive (2)	Anticipating (3)	Exploring (4)	Creative (5)
(1) Stage in Life-Cycle	late growth or maturity	early growth	late growth	emergence or decline	decline or emergence, or shift in stage
(2) Growth Rate	slow	accelerating	decelerating	fast (±)	discontinuous
(3) Change in Technology	slow	slow	fast	acceleration discontinuous familiar	discontinuous novel
(4) Change in Market Structure	slow	moderate	slow	discontinuous familiar	discontinuous novel
(5) Societal Pressures	none	moderate	strong	very strong	strong and novel
(6) Diversity of Technologies	none	low	moderate	high	high
(7) Demand for Growth Capital	low	high	moderate	very high	very high
(8) Profitability	high	high	moderate	low	low
(9) Rate of Technological Obsolescence	low	low	high	discontinuous	discontinuous
(10) Technological intensity	low	low	high	high	very high

Figure 5.8   Levels of Marketing Turbulence

Levels of Turbulence Attributes	Stable (1)	Reactive (2)	Anticipating (3)	Exploring (4)	Creative (5)
(1) Market Structure	monopoly	oligopoly	oligopoly	multi-compet	novel major entrants
(2) Customer Pressure	none	weak	strong	very strong	change in attitude
(3) Growth Rate	slow & stable	increasing/ stable	declining/ oscillating	fast/ oscillating	discontinuous
(4) Stage in Industry Life-Cycle	maturity/ decline	early growth	late growth	emergence/ decline	shift in stage
(5) Profitability	high	high	moderate	low	low
(6) Product Differentiation	none	low	moderate	high	products based on new technology
(7) Product Life-Cycles	long	long	short	short	short
(8) Frequency of New Products	very low	low	moderate	high	high novel products
(9) Economics of Scale	high	high	moderate	low	low
(10) Level of Capital intensity	high	high	moderate	low	low
(11) Critical Success Factors	market control	market share production costs	response to customer needs distribution service	anticipation of needs and opportunities	novel market-products; identific of hidden needs

of the marketing and entrepreneurial activity do not vary together. In fact, until the 1970s as the turbulence level of one activity rose the level of the other fell. For this reason, we have constructed two independent scales of marketing and entrepreneurial turbulence. These are shown in Figures 5.7 and 5.8. In a given industry the level of each can be diagnozed by first diagnozing the state of the respective attributes. This step will produce a profile in which not all entries will fall in one column. As a second step, the turbulence level of the environment can be identified by determining the mean value of the attributes.

Such procedure can only be useful if the profile of the attributes is fairly narrow and does not zig-zag across the table. This will occur if the attributes and values of Table 5.6 have been appropriately translated in Figures 5.7 and 5.8.

While during the past seventy years business turbulence has on the average been rising, the preceding discussion has shown that entrepreneurial and marketing turbulence do not necessarily move together. Nor do all industries move in step. We have already mentioned that a technological breakthrough, a structural change in the markets, or a political discontinuity may rapidly escalate turbulence in a stable industry or send a growing industry into decline. Thus, the environmental turbulence scale should be used as a tool for diagnosing the present and future turbulence of an industry, independently of the sequence shown in the table.

STRATEGIC THRUST

Figures 5.7 and 5.8 diagnose turbulence through the use of aggregate economic and technological data. Since turbulence is largely caused by behavior of the ESO in industry, an alternative approach is through observation of the strategic behavior of the ESO.

Definition: Strategic Thrust of an ESO is the set of characteristics which remain common to its strategic activity over time. In the language of the business planning literature, the strategic thrust is a *common thread* or the pattern of an ESOs strategy.

In Figure 5.9 we show five levels of thrust for the entrepreneurial and the marketing behavior. As the content of the figure shows, the differences among the entrepreneurial thrust lie in the degree to which they depart from the historical product-market-technology mix. The differences among the marketing thrusts lie in the aggressiveness with which the ESO does its marketing. For both thrusts 'discontinuity' represents bold and radical departures from past behavior.

Figure 5.8 is constructed so that the thrusts match the like-named levels of environmental turbulence. More precisely, this means that in an industry which has remained on one of the turbulence levels of Figure 5.7 for some time, *the largest percentage of ESOs* will use an entrepreneurial thrust described by a like-named column of Figure 5.9. In a similar manner, the columns of Figure 5.8 will match the *lines* of Figure 5.9.

ENTREPRENEURIAL \ MARKETING	CONTINUITY			DISCONTINUITY	
	STABLE	REACTIVE	ANTICIPATING	EXPLORING	CREATIVE
CONTINUITY — STABLE	FIXED PRODUCTS – MARKETS MAKING PRODUCT AVAILABLE TO MARKETS	EXPANSION OF FAMILIAR MARKETS INCREMENTAL PRODUCT ADAPTATION	EXPANSION TO RELATED MARKETS RELATED PRODUCT INNOVATION BASED ON KNOWN TECHNOLOGY	EXPANSION TO FOREIGN MARKETS NOVEL PRODUCT CONCEPTS ADOPTION OF NEW TECHNOLOGIES	OPENING NOVEL MARKETS PIONEERING PRODUCTS CREATION OF NOVEL TECHNOLOGIES
CONTINUITY — REACTIVE	DEFENSIVE MAINTENANCE OF MARKET SHARE				
CONTINUITY — ANTICIPATING	AGGRESSIVE SEARCH OF MARKET SHARE				
DISCONTINUITY — EXPLORING	ADOPTION OF NEW MARKETING CONCEPTS				
DISCONTINUITY — CREATIVE	PIONEERING MARKETING CONCEPTS				

Figure 5.9 Types of Strategic Thrust

The match between turbulence and thrust occurs only when the turbulence level has remained stable long enough to produce a steady pattern of strategic behavior. The situation during a shift of turbulence will be discussed in detail in a later chapter. While the match will be observed for the largest homogeneous group of ESOs in the industry, this group may or may not be the majority.

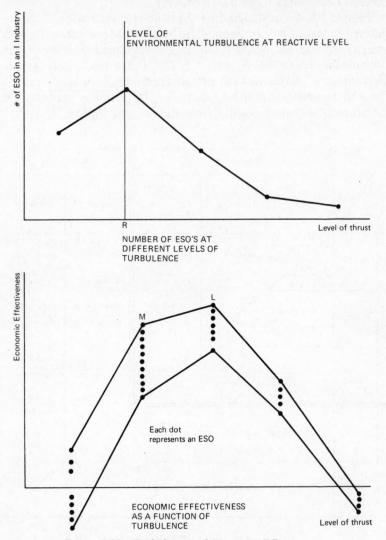

Figure 5.10   Turbulence and Economic Effectiveness

These are the ESOs that are 'tuned in' to the environment. Many others will be 'out of tune' to various degrees. We are hypothesizing that the strategic thrusts of the remainder will be distributed in a continuous manner, illustrated in the upper part of Figure 5.10. The figure depicts the distribution of thrusts in an industry whose turbulence level is *R*. The largest number of ESOs use the reactive thrust. The greater the distance of a thrust from the majority thrust, the fewer ESOs will be found pursuing it.

In the lower part of Figure 5.10 we show the distribution of economic effectiveness (ROI) which corresponds to the thrust distribution in the upper part. The curve incorporates three hypotheses. The first is that the maximum return goes not to the average behavior, but to a strategic thrust which is modestly ahead of the average. This is commonly observable in business industries where the leaders are enough, but not too far, ahead of the crowd to capture the market. The firms which 'stick their neck out' by making premature innovations perform poorly, so do those that lag behind the majority. Thus the second hypothesis is that the further the thrust of an ESO is from the optimum, the lower will be its average effectiveness.

The third hypothesis is illustrated by the range in economic effectiveness at a given thrust shown in the lower part of Figure 5.10, where each dot represents a different ESO. This is a 'residual' hypothesis, which holds that differences between thrust and turbulence explain only a part of the differences in economic effectiveness of an ESO. We have already identified one such 'residual' factor as the critical mass factor *S*. In succeeding sections we shall be discovering other 'residuals'. For the moment, we characterize them by a factor *K*. We can compress the preceding hypotheses into the following short-hand formula:

$$ROI_{te} = ROI_{ee} . \alpha_{te} . S.P.K$$

where

ROI_{te} is the economic effectivness of an ESO when it uses thrust t in an environment on turbulence level e;

ROI_{ee} is the maximum possible effectiveness of thrust e in an environment e;

α_{te} is a thrust effectiveness factor.

Translated into words, the formula implies the following
hypotheses:

HYPOTHESIS 5.6: DISTRIBUTION OF STRATEGIC THRUST
In an environment of steady turbulence, the strategic thrust of
the largest group of ESOs will match the turbulence level. But
many others will have thrusts above and below the level.

HYPOTHESIS 5.7: EFFECTIVENESS OF THRUST
The maximum economic effectiveness is reached by an ESO
whose thrust is moderately ahead of the turbulence level. The
effectiveness of other thrusts varies inversely as their distance
from the optimum.

EFFECT OF THE RULES OF THE GAME

In Figure 5.11 we compare distributions of behavior of a for-
profit business industry to a non-profit industry. The upper solid
line shows that all types of strategic thrust are likely to be found in

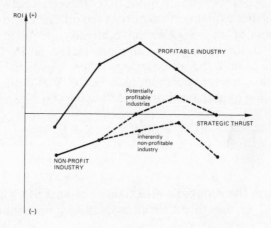

*Figure 5.11   Economic Effectiveness of Business and
Non-Profit Industries*

a for-profit industry and a majority of firms realize a positive economic result. The lower short solid line illustrates a typical non-profit industry in which strategic behavior is limited to stable and reactive thrusts, and the economic results are negative.

As we have already discussed in dealing with environmental dependence, the differences between the two curves come from the *rules of the game* under which the two types of institution operate in society. The positive performance of the business firm is ascribable, first, to the strong survival pressure – negative performers don't last long – and to the historical freedom of the firm to choose its strategic thrust. The opposite applies to non-profits: they are under a weak survival pressure and their choice of the thrust is usually severely circumscribed.

It is usual to set up a non-profit to deliver a very specific service, specified in the charter, which, in our language, limits the ESO to stable or at best to reactive entrepreneurial behavior. In many instances, non-profits are set up for areas of social need which cannot sustain a profit-seeking business approach, because the costs of delivering the service exceed the price which could be obtained in the open market. Thus even if the non-profits were to be strongly motivated to perform (say, by making their subsidies dependent on performance), and even if their managements were given full freedom of strategic choice, the performance would still remain negative (see the lower dashed extension of the non-profit curve labelled 'inherently non-profit industry'.)

But there are areas of social need in which non-profits could become economically effective if the constraints on strategic freedom were removed – for example, the Amtrack Corporation, whose mission to provide medium-distance passenger transportations is limited by charter to doing so by means of rail, which makes Amtrack unprofitable. Alongside Amtrack, there are several bus companies and feeder airlines which profitably fill the identical mission. Similarly, alongside the U. S. Post Office, there are several mail-carrying companies which make significant profits.

It is ironic that in both of our examples the U. S. Government has recently given for-profit status to both Amtrack and the Post Office without giving them the strategic freedom necessary to achieve a profitable status. It is not our purpose, however, to argue in this book that these organizations should be given wider strategic freedoms, nor that, with freedom, the two bureaucracies could be converted into profitable enterprises. The point of the discussion is to underline the inconsistency in rules of the game, which, at the same time, deprive an ESO of the necessary strategic freedom and insist that it make a profit.

Such inconsistency in regulation has already converted some business industries from profitable to inherently unprofitable ones. As we discussed previously, since early in the twentieth century a progressively growing number of rules of the game has been used by society. Some of these, such as protective legislation, served to enhance the profitability of the industry. But many others depressed it, either through limiting the strategic behavior (e.g. safety and automotive pollution legislation), or price regulation, or through increasing the costs of doing business (e.g. industrial pollution, or strip-mining legislation).

A lively conflict has raged for many years between proponents of 'laissez faire', who argued that the cumulative constraints would destroy the profitability of the free enterprise, and regulationists who argued that 'economic freedom is too important to be left to business managers'.

Constraints have proliferated and business has, on the whole, shown an amazing resilience in coping with them and remaining profitable. There is, however, the extreme example of an over-constrained firm found in socialist economies, which has been chronically economically inefficient. Thus somewhere on the scale of constraints between laissez-faire and the firm in the Soviet Union under that Stalinist regime, there is a point at which an industry becomes inherently unprofitable.

The rules of the game are part of the residual factor K discussed in the last section which modifies the profitability of a strategic thrust. If we now redefine the ROI_{ee} as the maximum effectiveness of thrust e in an environment e, *which is free from political constraints*, we can rewrite the formula:

$$ROI_{te} = ROI_{ee} \cdot \alpha_{te} \cdot S \cdot P \cdot R$$

where P is the impact of the political rules of the game;
and R is a new 'residual' which we shall be discussing presently.

On the basis of the preceding discussion, we advance the following hypotheses:

HYPOTHESIS 5.8: IMPACT OF RULES OF THE GAME
The rules of the game imposed on an industry affect the level of economic effectiveness of the ESO within it.

HYPOTHESIS 5.9: REASONS FOR UNPROFITABILITY
An industry may be unprofitable, either because the demand area which it serves is inherently unprofitable, or because the rules of the game make it so.

For the last hypothesis, we borrow a term introduced by Peter Broden.

HYPOTHESIS 5.10: STRATEGIC TRAP
For every industry which shows positive economic effectiveness under 'laissez-faire' conditions, there is a configuration of constraints which will make the industry inherently unprofitable. We shall call such configuration of rules a *strategic trap*.

Under such configuration, the factor P in the preceding equation becomes negative.

6 Strategic Capability

'First we shape our structures, and afterwards they shape us.'
Winston Churchill

OPENNESS OF BEHAVIOR

Shifting attention inward from the environment to the workings of the ESO, we encounter two traditional models. One, found in microeconomic literature, describes the business firm as restless, aggressive and continuously seeking to maximize profit. The second model, used by organizational sociologists, depicts both firms and non-profits, at best, as passive, reacting to events, lacking rationality, 'muddling through' from one event to another. At its worst, sociologists see ESOs as bureaucratic, introverted, resisting change, seeking to isolate themselves from the environment.

Our discussion of strategic thrust has shown that the above models represent two extremes between which lies a range of behaviors. In dealing with the inner workings of ESOs, we shall use the same approach by introducing intermediate models of behavior, which are, in fact the most common ones. To do this, we borrow from systems theory the concept of organizational openness.

Definition: Organizational Openness is a property of an ESO which is jointly determined by:
1. The *information perspective*, which describes the futurity and the novelty of the information which an ESO uses in its work.
2. The *action perspective*, which describes the familiarity of an ESOs current actions with respect to its past experiences.

We illustrate the concept of information perspective by examples observable in practice:

72

1. Many ESOs, both public and private, rely on historically familiar information. The information used by management is usually stale, processed by the accounting system from past operational results: the sales already made, the patients already treated, the students already enrolled, etc. Familiar repetitive patterns of information are held valid, unexplained deviations from the familiar are regarded as computational errors or temporary abberations, rather than as signs of a changing environment.

2. Another group of ESOs attempts to live in the present by removing the staleness from the accounting information. They develop quick-responding information systems which reduce the lag between events and reports. They also seek information directly from the environment through surveys, economic data, etc. But they, like the preceding group, place a high value on historical patterns and relationships. 'Intuition' and 'experience' are key words in the vocabulary of such ESOs.

3. A substantial and growing percentage of ESOs, particularly business firms, look to the future and try to anticipate new developments in the environment. A majority seeks to recognize familiar patterns in future events. Their forecasts are usually extrapolative, typically optimistic, based on the assumption that the future world will be an enlarged and improved version of the past.

4. A small percentage of future-oriented ESOs do not make the assumption that the future will be a smooth extrapolation of the familiar past. They search the environment for significant departures which will change future trends and introduce discontinuities.

5. Another small percentage are what may be called 'information creators'. Their search of the environment is less for 'what will be' and more for 'what can be.' They seek new patterns of events which can be brought about by deliberate action.

The second characteristic of openness, the action perspective, will generally match the information perspective:

1. The backward-looking ESOs prefer alternatives which succeeded in the past. Change from precedent is suspect and to be avoided. 'The way we do things around here is . . .' is a phrase in common usage. Behavior is aimed at preserving the historical relation to environment: historical products, markets, marketing approaches, product technology, etc.

2. ESOs which live in the present are prepared to depart from the past as long as the departures are consistent with and not greatly different from past experience. While incremental departures from the past are acceptable, they are neither sought nor welcomed. 'We are prepared to roll with the punches' is the common phrase.

3. ESOs which extrapolate into the future seek to predict threats and opportunities. Their attitude toward the environment is proactive. They search for new departures, instead of waiting for new events to overtake them. However, these ESOs will test the validity of their options by traditional *and tested perceptions and models of the world.* Acceptable alternatives must be a logical extension of past experience. To identify and explore the future, many ESOs of this type use long-range planning systems. The slogan is to 'plan ahead'.

4. ESOs which go beyond extrapolation to perceive new worlds and discontinuities seek novel as well as unfamiliar opportunities. Events at variance with experience are not rejected. On the contrary, new images of the future tend to be preferred to the 'old worn-out ways' of doing things. Models of the world which are limited to past experience alone are suspect of myopia. The slogans may be 'No man is an island' and 'Be where the action is.'

5. The information-creators are also action-creators. They seek markets which have never been served, human needs which have not yet been filled, new juxtapositions of needs and technologies. 'Invent the future' is their motto.

We have summarized the characteristics of openness in Figure 6.1. We use the same column headings as for strategic thrust (see Figure 5.9), because the two are mirror images of each other. When the openness and thrust are matched, the view of the world captures the information necessary for making the thrust fully effective. A level of openness lower than the thrust will deprive the ESO of essential information about environmental threats and opportunities. A higher level, as we shall see later, will set up a tendency to raise the level of thrust.

A superficial comparison of the five levels of behavior may leave the impression that open behaviors on the right of Figure 6.1 are 'good' and closed behaviors on the left are 'bad'. The stable state is easily identified with classical conservative 'bureaucracy', which has become a pejorative term in the

ORGANIZATIONAL OPENNESS / ATTRIBUTE	STABLE	REACTIVE	ANTICIPATORY	EXPLORING	CREATIVE
INFORMATION PERSPECTIVE	PAST	PAST	FUTURE EXTRAPOLATED	FUTURE GLOBAL	FUTURE GLOBAL
ACTION PERSPECTIVE	REPETITION OF FAMILIAR EXPERIENCE	INCREMENTAL CHANGE IN PAST EXPERIENCE	NEW ALTERNATIVES PREDICTABLE FROM PAST	NEW COMBINATIONS OF FAMILIAR EXPERIENCE	NOVEL ALTERNATIVES

Figure 6.1 Levels of Organizational Openness

industrial culture; the entrepreneurial change-seeking creative states are identified with progress and growth. These perceptions are rooted in social norms developed in the Industrial Age when the social priority was on raising the level of society's economic welfare, and when economic growth and strategic aggressiveness were dominant social values.

Reflecting these norms, there has been a tendency in both sociological and business literature of the past thirty years to prescribe behavior in the 'open' modes. But society's values and norms are changing. Economic growth is no longer the only criterion of social progress. Other values have already emerged such as, for example, the responsibility of ESOs for providing satisfying and personally fulfilling employment. For a large proportion of individuals, living on the razor's edge of uncertainty, which is typical of open ESOs, is a psychologically frightening condition.

Further, as we have already discussed in matching strategic thrust to turbulence, wide open behavior leads to best economic results only when the level of environmental turbulence is comparably high. As we have seen, much of the economic growth of the United States between 1900 and 1930 was brought about by stable/reactive strategic behaviors.

We need, therefore, to explore further both what determines openness and how openness affects performance. The determinants of openness are two: the strategic culture of the ESO, which we shall treat in the next chapter, and the strategic capability, which we discuss next.

MANAGERIAL CAPABILITY

In a small organization the range of possible responses and of behavior is determined by the personal skills, knowledge and motivation of one or two key individuals.

As an organization grows, *group* skills, knowledge and values are developed which are more than a simple sum of the participants' contributions. When the organization becomes large, the work groups multiply and yet another ingredient of capability is added which is determined by the manner in which group interact and complement one another. We shall call the resulting collective competence the *organizational capability* of an ESO.

In small ESOs, managerial capability is undifferentiated. As an ESO grows, and if its various logistic functions remain technologically undifferentiated, a managerial structure develops based on hierarchical authority relations. Managers are distinguished from one another by the level they occupy in the hierarchy.

In technologically intensive and differentiated ESOs, particularly in manufacturing firms, a different pattern of evolution occurred during the past hundred years. A historical milestone, early in this century, was the emergence of the *functional form* of organization, which, to paraphrase from Du Pont history, put 'like' functions together. These functions were production, marketing, research and development, and finance. Similarly, in hospitals, the functions of doctors, nurses, laboratories, housekeeping, etc. became grouped together. In the university the grouping developed according to the disciplines of the faculty.

Each functional grouping requires special capabilities on the part of its managers: an understanding of the underlying technology, of the particular work processes, of the values which motivate the doers, skills in designing work, and in managing the workers. Consequently, a class of specialist-managers emerged, whose qualifications were based on the skills in managing a specific function. These managers formed the middle and lower levels of the hierarchy.

At the top levels of hierarchy, managers were charged with coordinating the functional work and particularly with guiding and controlling the behavior of the enterprise as a whole. These levels became known as *general management*.

Thus managerial capability can be subdivided into *functional* capability, which applies to guidance and control of the respective logistic functions, and a *general management* capability which applies to guidance of the enterprise as a whole.

GENERAL MANAGEMENT COMPETENCE

General management capability is determined by two factors. The first is what we shall call the *competence*, which is the range of skills that an ESO can bring to its strategic behavior. The second is the *capacity*, which is the volume of the strategic work that it can deliver.

For discussion of competence, we follow our standard procedure by constructing several competence profiles which are matched to different strategic thrusts. These profiles are shown in Figure 6.2. The respective profiles are optimum for the strategic thrusts which carry the corresponding name in Figure 5.9. Each level is described by a configuration of eight observable organizational attributes.

A key attribute is the problem-solving approach, encompassing individual skills, personal knowledge, as well as group dynamics. The differences among problem-solving behaviors lie in the manner in which the process is triggered, the method of analysis used, and the scope of alternatives considered. As the figure shows, the behavior ranges from reaction to problems which have already affected the ESO to anticipation, to invention of new opportunities through a creative search.

The respective problem-solving approaches have been described in the literature of different disciplines. Organizational sociologists and political scientists have studies the stable/reactive behavior. The classical descriptions have been provided by Cyert and March from the sociological point of view ('problemistic' problem-solving), and Lindbloom ('muddling through') from the political. Virtually all of mathematical-analytic approches to problem-solving are based on the assumption of optimum-seeking anticipating behavior. Sociologists (Simon) have also studied the ill-structured approaches, and psychologists made important contributions to creative problem-solving.

Important differences among problem-solving styles are found at the stage of analysis. In the stable mode, alternatives are considered one at a time, evaluated by comparisons to past experience, and tested in practice. If the trial fails, another alternative is introduced. The process stops after the first success – a characteristic which led Herbert Simon to call such problem-solving 'satisficing'.

Reactive problem-solving seeks to correct deficiencies through systematic analysis of the causes. The process is also typically satisficing.

As its name suggests, the anticipating mode tries to predict problems. It is an analytic process in which an effort is made to identify all possible alternatives and establish explicit and quan-

Figure 6.2 Profiles of General Management Competence

Level of behavior Attributes	Stable	Reactive	Anticipating	Exploring	Creative
(a) Problem Solving	Problem-triggered Trial and Error Satisficing	Problem-triggered Diagnostic Satisficing	Anticipatory Well-structured Optimizing	Anticipatory Ill-structured	Creative Ill-structured
(b) Process	Follows structure			Follows problem logic	
(c) Leadership Attributes	Custodial persuasive	Disciplinary persuasive	Growth-directing inspiring	Charismatic entrepreneurial	Creative charismatic
(d) Management Information	Past-precedents	Past performance	Future based on past trends	Future departures and discontinuities	Possible new futures New juxtapositions
(e) Organizational Structure	Functional	Functional	Divisional	Multinational, matrix	New ventures, Project management
(f) Environmental Surveillance	None	None	Extrapolative forecasting	Trend analysis, techno-socio-demographic forecasts	Major discontinuities, scenarios, futures invention
(g) Management System	Policy and Procedure Manuals	Control, capital budgeting, management by objectives	Long-range planning, budgeting	Strategic planning, PPBS	Venture management, Strategic Issue, Analysis, Brainstorming
(h) Management Science	Work Study, Equipment Replacement, Matching loading	Financial Ratio Analysis, Capital Investment Analysis	Operations Research, Computerized transaction analysis	'What if modelling', Acquisition analysis, Impact analysis, Delphi, Scenarios, Technological Sociological-Political forcasting	Synectics, Creative behavior, Innovative behavior

tified relations among variables. The probable outcomes of the alternatives are computed and the best ('optimal') alternative is selected.

In the exploring and creative problem-solving, a major effort is centered on identifying the nature of the problem and identifying or creating new alternatives. The set of alternatives is never complete, the structure is typically ill-defined. The alternatives may be singular, as in the case of very tough problems, or multiple. The choice is typically made by testing each alternative against several, usually incompatible, criteria.

As Figure 6.2 shows, anticipatory, exploring, and creative problem-solving are usually organized according to the logic of the problem. Whenever the logic crosses organizational lines, the formal organization is disregarded in favor of informal 'task-forces' or cross-departmental teams. By contrast, stable and reactive processes follow the hierarchy of the formally established organization. Communication is through formal channels. problems are assigned to departments and solutions are reported back to the originator.

A third key attribute of general management capability is the leadership attributes used in both problem-solving and subsequent strategic action. As can be seen from line (c) of Figure 6.2, the first three levels of capability calls for skills in marshalling and directing social energy along a historically experienced path. Exploring and creative leadership both require a higher-order social skill: the 'pied piper' charisma to lead the ESO into uncharted and untried directions. In addition to social skills, exploring and creative leaders must also contribute the substance of the creative alternatives which they propose to follow. (See discussion of strategic leadership in Chapter 9.)

A fourth key element of competence, shown in line (d), is the information available to management. The stable/reactive competences are backward-looking, while the other three are progressively forward-oriented. Item (d) has an obvious similarity to the information perspective of the preceding section. As we shall see later, the two are not necessarily identical in an ESO: it is possible to have an information system which is forward-looking and a management with a backward-looking information perspective.

Lines (a), (b), (c) and (d) describe what might be called *informal* attributes of the competence. They are observable through inquiry and observation, but they are not explicitly formalized or systematized within an ESO. In large and medium-sized ESOs, particularly in business firms, a number of formal arrangements for doing managerial work have emerged during the past eighty years. These are illustrated in lines (e) and (f).

The universally used method for organizing work is through specifications of task-authority-responsibility roles and relationships, which is called *organizational structure*. We have already mentioned the functional form as the first major organizing concept which emerged in the 1910s. In the 1920s business firms poineered with the divisional concept, and after World War II multinational and matrix structures emerged.

Typically, a structure attempts to accommodate two logics: the logic of managerial work and the logic of the logistic work, each of which may call for a different structure. For this reason, the structure attribute is a weak correlate of the level of managerial competence. For example, in firms in the petrochemical industry general management competence is usually at the anticipating level, but the organization is functional because of the imperatives of petrochemical process technology.

Attributes (f) and (g) describe, respectively, formal arrangements for getting environmental information into an ESO, and for conducting managerial problem-solving. Shown in the respective columns are the most sophisticated systems now available for the respective levels of managerial competence. The systems are not substitutes for each other but are complementary. Thus a sophisticated firm with a strategic planning system is also likely to have well-developed long-range planning, management control, and policies and procedure manuals.

Systems are a very strong correlate of managerial competence. An established and culturally accepted system forces the entire organization into behavior prescribed by the system.

The final line of Figure 6.2 deals with computational and analytic tools used for improvement of managerial problem-solving. They illustrate the capabilities typically found in sophisticated business firms at each of the respective levels of competence.

When the values of several attributes fall into the same column, they form a vector of mutually supporting attributes. Thus in a stable mode organizational problem-solving seeks to change the ESO as little as possible; the rigid structure compartmentalizes and isolates problem-solving activities; the system is static, composed of standard procedures, the unstructured surveillance system relies on common wisdom and personal experience. As one progresses from left to right in the figure, the respective matching attributes become increasingly flexible, dynamic, and environmentally oriented to support an increasingly venturesome strategic thrust.

The informal problem-solving styles described in lines (a) through (d) evolved partly in response to changes in environmental turbulence, and partly in response to the leadership styles of key managers. The management technology described in lines (e) through (h) developed as managers sought to rationalize and improve the problem-solving behavior. This process has been one of invention, trial and error.

The management technology shown in respective columns is 'state of the art' found in progressive business firms. Historically the competence of non-profits was limited to the informal attributes (a) through (e). Today, technology is increasingly used by firms and has begun to penetrate the non-profits. In the latter, Management by Objectives (MBO) and Planning Programming Budgetting System (PPBS) have the most popular technologies.

In each column of Figure 6.2 the respective attributes are mutually complementary for supporting a particular mode of strategic behavior. If the strategic thrust of the ESO remains stable long enough, the individual attributes develop to match one another. But under changing turbulence, when the thrust is also changing, it is not uncommon for the respective attributes to become unbalanced. For example, today's turbulence is forcing management increasingly to deal with strategic surprises, but the systems for doing so are just emerging.

Another typical cause of unbalances are changes introduced by new top management when it takes over an ESO. Rather than shift the entire competence vector, new management typically puts emphasis on changes which are supportive of its own management style. We illustrate this in Figure 6.3 where we examine the now famous 'Macnamara impact' on the U.S. Defense Department. As shown, Mr Macnamara inherited an essentially reactive competence which was not responsive to the highly turbulent challenges posed by environment. A highly rational and incisive decision maker, Macnamara focused his efforts on installing a sophisticated management system (PPBS), supported by the technology of systems analysis. However, the

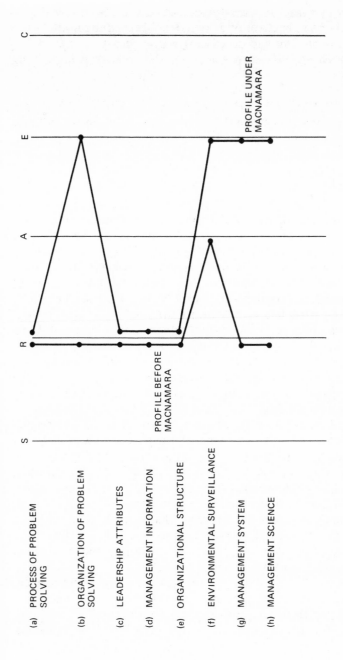

S   R   A   E   C

(a) PROCESS OF PROBLEM SOLVING

(b) ORGANIZATION OF PROBLEM SOLVING

(c) LEADERSHIP ATTRIBUTES

(d) MANAGEMENT INFORMATION

(e) ORGANIZATIONAL STRUCTURE

(f) ENVIRONMENTAL SURVEILLANCE

(g) MANAGEMENT SYSTEM

(h) MANAGEMENT SCIENCE

PROFILE UNDER MACNAMARA

PROFILE BEFORE MACNAMARA

Figure 6.3 'Macnamara's Impact' on General Management of the U.S. Defense Department

other key elements of the competence of the defense establishment remained reactive, and impeded Macnamara's efforts to introduce exploring and creative strategic thrust.

The above discussion is based on the following underlying hypothesis:

HYPOTHESIS 6.1: THRUST-COMPETENCE MATCH
For each strategic thrust there is a combination of competence attributes which is most effective for supporting the thrust.

LOGISTIC COMPETENCE

The strategic responsibility of general management is to be tuned and responsive to the ambient environment, to identify and understand quickly the implications of change, to determine courses of action to be taken, and to guide their implementation. The strategic responsibility of functional management is to implement the strategic thrust: to build new plant and facilities, to develop new products, to reorganize the productive and marketing processess, to produce pilot quantities, and to establish them on the market. This process involves a large number of work-receivers: production workers, salesmen, laboratory technicians, researchers, doctors, teachers, nurses, etc. We shall refer to the ability to carry out this complex series of actions as the *logistic competence* of an ESO.

We have seen that management competence is 'thrust-specific' in the sense that: (1) each type of thrust calls for a different configuration of attributes, and (2) the same thrust-competence match combination applies across a range of very different industries. Thus the general management of the U.S. space effort is quite similar to that of an aggressive firm.

Logistic competence for strategic change is, in the first place 'technology-specific'. Thus the technological know-how of a Xerox would not be applicable to a leading pharmaceutical company, such as, say, Hoffman Laroche.

But, beyond the content of the scientific and technological know-how, logistic competence is also thrust-specific, because a given level of thrust requires a generic combination of logistic processes. We demonstrate this in two steps. First, in Figure 6.4, we show a generic list of know-how, skills, knowledge, and

Figure 6.4 Attributes of Logistic Competence

Type of work Contributor	Operations	Marketing	Entrepreneurship
Management	Work management Union-management relations Production management Production control Financial planning and control Production planning Work study Investment Analysis Budgeting and control system design Budgeting Performance diagnosis Plant layout and design	Long-term planning Promotion and advertising planning Salesmen deployment Sales analysis Salesmen management Competitive analysis Forecasting Growth financing	Strategic planning Project management Management of creative work R & D Planning Venture management Planning system design Impact Analysis Impact Analysis Trend Analysis Investment Risk Analysis
Technocracy	* Plant * Inventories * Distribution facilities Machinery and equipment Production know-how Process know-how Distribution skills	Sales Selling Advertising Promotion Customer financing	* Laboratories * Research and development * Equipment Research skills Development skills

* Denotes capital-intensive items

specialized facilities which are found in an ESO. We base the list on a manufacturing firm (and use its language), because it has the greatest diversity of logistic elements. But through elimination of inapplicable items and translation of some terms, Figure 6.4 can be transferred to describe the logistic process in any ESO.

As the second step we show in Figure 6.5 the particular profiles of competence required for success of generic strategic thrusts. As the figure shows, in the 'closed' states the key competence is operations, since marketing and entrepreneurship are rudimentary and not essential to success. (We recall our earlier example of Henry Ford I's definition of success: 'Give it to them any color, so long as it is black.') Marketing competence becomes a central process for the anticipating thrust. Entrepreneurship is the key process for exploring and creative ESOs.

Again we note that the columns of Figure 6.5 represent balanced profiles which offer optimum support to the respective strategic thrusts. As with general management competence, we would frequently expect to encounter cases of unbalanced logistic profiles.

HYPOTHESIS 6.2: LOGISTIC COMPETENCE AND STRATEGIC THRUST

The effectiveness of a particular logistic competence profile in supporting a strategic thrust depends on:
1. The match of the profile to the thrust;
2. The quality and the relevance of technology available in the ESO to the demands of the market place.

STRATEGIC CAPACITY

The logistic and the general management competences determine the quality of an ESOs strategic work. However, an excellent but miniscule competence may be just as inadequate as a large but irrelevant competence. Therefore the potential *quantity* of work needs to be discussed next.

In the past, few efforts have been made to measure general management capacity. In part this was due to a mystique which has surrounded general management, according to which general management was an intangible, esoteric, entrepreneurial activity which defied systematization and measurement. In part the lack

Figure 6.5 Profiles of Logistic Competence

Levels of Strategic Thrust / Function	S	R	A	E	S
Key Management Function	Operations		Entrepreneurship		
Entrepreneurship	Process Improvement	Product improvement	Marketing New Products/ Processes	Technology Adaptation	New Technology Development
Operations	Repetitive Operations	Complex Operations Control	Expansion of Operations	Integration of New Technology	Technology Changeover
Marketing	Product Distribution	Selling	Promotion/ Advertising	New Marketing Concepts	New Ventures
Finance	Accounting	Financial Control	Financial Planning Capital Investment	Financing of Growth	Major New Risk Management

of interest in management capacity stemmed from the *minimal management principle*. This principle was an outgrowth of a wave of decentralization of managerial authority which swept American industry around the mid-century. Given prominence by Ralph Cordiner and Walter Smiddy of the General Electric Co., the principle states that general management should delegate the maximum possible amount of work to the operating levels. As a result, the *smallness* of the general management group became a criterion of the quality of general management.

The principle was valid for its time, when the level of environmental turbulence was relatively low and the amount of strategic work small enough to be handled at lower levels alongside the day-to-day operating workload. As the environment became increasingly turbulent, the volume and importance of strategic work grew and with it the size of general management. Today, in the same General Electric Company there is a sizeable general management group which devotes its exclusive attention to strategic work. There is also a visible trend in many other large corporations toward a recentralization of certain key strategic responsibilities, particularly those concerned with the overall strategic balance of the enterprise.

Among the components of the logistic competence the most difficult to measure is the capacity of research and development activity. The business practice, which is generally recognized as unsatisfactory, has been to allocate a certain percentage of past year's sales to the next year's R & D budget. The anomaly of this practice is self-evident: it results in reduced R & D budgets during periods of falling sales – exactly the period during which R & D needs to be enhanced!

The marketing capacity is somewhat easier to estimate through the size of the sales force and coverage of territory.

The best logistic capacity measurement is in operations, since techniques are available for sizing the plant, the equipment and the personnel requirements as a function of the physical volume of the planned throughput.

HYPOTHESIS 6.3: ORGANIZATIONAL CAPACITY

The organizational capacity needed to support the strategic work of an ESO is proportional to:
1. The level of the strategic thrust;
2. The size of the strategic budget.

DYNAMICS OF STRATEGIC CAPABILITY

We can now define strategic capability.

Definition: Strategic Capability is a measure of effectiveness of an ESO in supporting a particular thrust. It is determined by:
1. General management competence profile and capacity;
2. Logistic competence profile and capacity;
3. The range and quality of the ESOs technology.

The strategic capability is optimal when all competence components match the strategic thrust, when the capacity is adequately matched to the strategic budget, and when the technology is the best available for meeting the demands of the market place.

As discussed above, strategic capability of an ESO is frequently suboptimal. This may be the result of a mismatch of managerial and logistic capacities, which occurs when the heritage of the minimum management principle prevents building of an adequate management capacity, with the result that the logistic capacity of the ESO exceeds the general management capacity. Suboptimality may also be due to a mismatch among the competence components, or to obsolescence of an ESOs technology.

In many other cases the entire capability vector is suboptimal because of failures on the part of an ESO to make a timely adaptation to a changed strategic thrust. A fundamental insight into this lag phenomenon has been provided by A. D. Chandler in his seminal book *Strategy and Structure*. Chandler has shown that in the first half of the twentieth century, adaptation of ESOs to changing turbulence followed a typical pattern. The first to occur was a shift in the level of environmental turbulence. An adjustment in the strategic thrust followed, with a time lag. After another time lag a shift followed in the capability.

The shift in capability was typically unplanned and piecemeal. A change in structure had usually been the first step. When this proved insufficient, other components of the competence profile followed: change in information, in problem-solving skills, in style of leadership, etc.

Chandler's results show that such a sequential and piecemeal approach was slow and inefficient; so slow, in fact, that frequently firms were still completing a previous adaption when a new change in turbulence made another adaptation necessary. As a result, during the first half of the century, in many firms the environment, thrust and capability remained permanently misaligned in the manner shown by Curve *A* in Figure 6.6.

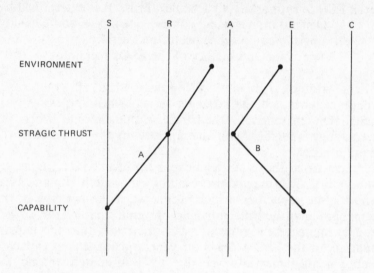

A – LAGGING THRUST AND CAPABILITY
B – LEADING CAPABILITY, LAGGING THRUST

Figure 6.6   Alignment of ESO with Environment

After World War Two, the pattern began to change. As we have already discussed in Chapter 5, the level of organizational intelligence rose rapidly. Management technology became popular, thanks to the influence of business schools, the growing number of books, periodicals and management seminars. This speeded up the dissemination of advanced management technology developed by pioneering firms. Academics who brought engineering, physics, mathematics and economics to the study of management, also began to invent new technologies. These new technologies became a status symbol synonymous with good management.

As a result, firms confronted with new environmental turbulence increasingly began to reach for a new systems and new structure, such as computer technology, as the initial response to their difficulty. For example, in the 1950s, both business firms and the federal government reached for the technologies of long-range and strategic planning as a miracle solution for coping with turbulence. In the late 1960s hospitals and universities joined this trend.

Thus, the Chandlerian sequence began to reverse itself. Instead of adapting the strategic thrust, ESOs began with adaptation of the capability. Thus the environment-thrust-capability imbalance was reversed in the manner shown by curve *B* of Figure 6.6.

But, as in the past, the new solutions were introduced in a piecemeal fashion. It was typical, for example, to install a long-range planning system without developing an appropriate environmental surveillance system, or training managers in new methods of problem-solving. The result was a dual imbalance.: first, between the strategic thrust and the system, and second, between the system and the other components of capability.

The new tools frequently appeared threatening to managers who did not understand them, did not know how to use them, and felt that the tool exposed their incompetence. If the new system was maintained by the authority of top management long enough to force managers to learn to live with the new tool, other components of capability developed to support the system, and the new capability produced a new strategic thrust. Thus the Chandlerian sequence was reversed and 'strategy followed structure'.

But if the managerial support was removed too early, in many cases the system atrophied to the level consistent with the historical strategic thrust. This has occurred in numerous efforts to introduce strategic planning into business firms and PPBS into government organizations. In the former case the regression was typically back to long-range planning, and in the latter to budgeting. A dramatic example of the latter occurred in the U.S. Department of Defense when Mr Macnamara left office.

In other cases the new technology remained in place after top management support weakened, but it was isolated from the ongoing work of the ESO. In many firms, long-range planning became an 'annual exercise in frustration' and had little impact on strategic work outside the planning period. In many other firms management science staffs continued to turn out new mathematical models which remained unheeded by management.

But with all of its shortcomings, the reversal of the 'strategy-structure' sequence is an important historical milestone. As discussed in Chapter 5, the time available for organizational response is shrinking. The 'structure-strategy' sequence reduces the time needed for response and thus enables ESOs to cope with decreasing predictability. It is safe to predict that in the future ESOs will increasingly turn to building a flexible strategic capability in advance of changes in the environment.

HYPOTHESIS 6.4: REVERSAL OF CHANDLERIAN SEQUENCE

1. Today, a large percentage of ESOs continues to behave in the stable/reactive mode in which adjustment of strategic thrust follows a change in turbulence, and adjustment of capability 'follows' the thrust.
2. In the future, ESOs will increasingly eliminate the environment-thrust lag through strategic planning, and will also reverse the thrust-capability sequence.

MODEL OF STRATEGIC PERFORMANCE POTENTIAL

We can now pull together key variables that affect the economic effectiveness of an ESO. In the preceding chapter we advanced hypotheses on the relationship between environmental turbulence and strategic thrust. In essence these stated that for every level of strategic thrust there is a corresponding maximum economic effectiveness (ROI) possible in the environment. Thus:

1. When the thrust of an ESO is matched to the environmental average (i.e., when the ESO behaves like the majority), its maximum potential will be at point M on Figure 5.9.
2. When an ESO behaves more aggressively, but not too far above the environmental turbulence, it can become one of the most successful members of the industry (point L on Figure 5.9).

We recall further the meaning of the word 'potential' used above. As discussed previously, strategic activity 'brings in the sales' but the potential of these sales may or may not be realized by the operating activity.

In this chapter we have first identified openness of behavior as the internal counterpart of the strategic thrust. We have further hypothesized that the effectiveness of the strategic thrust is determined by the match between the thrust and the strategic competence of the ESO. When the competence matches the thrust, the ESO has the best chance of obtaining the maximum ROI which is available to the particular thrust in the environment. When there is a mismatch, the effectiveness of the thrust will be reduced in proportion to the degree of mismatch.

Figure 6.7   Competence Effectiveness Coefficients
(β_{ct}) for Strategic Thrust

Strategic Thrust Strategic Competence	S	R	A	I	C
S	1	0.5	0	−1.0	−1.5
R	0.5	1	0.5	0	−1.0
A	0	0.5	1	0.5	0
I	−1	0	0.5	1	0.5
C	−1.5	−1.0	0	0.5	1

We illustrate this phenomenon in Figure 6.7 by means of a *competence effectiveness coefficient*. The values assigned to the coefficient are judgemental and should not be regarded as empirically established. As the figure shows, when the thrust and the competence match the coefficient is unity. As the mismatch increases, the coefficient decreases. We are hypothesizing, in fact, that when the gap is large enough the wrong competence will render the thrust totally ineffective. This can be seen in the first line, for example, where a stable competence will produce zero results for an anticipatory strategic thrust and losses for inquiring and creative behavior. These are the cases of a bureaucratic system frustrating and distorting efforts by the leadership. This occurred for example, when the U.S. military establishment frustrated President Kennedy's order to remove offensive missiles from Turkey during the Cuban missile crisis.

We note that the reverse mismatch is equally unsatisfactory, as demonstrated by the first column. An example here is one we cited earlier of the failure of aggressive conglomerate managers to run conservative subsidiaries, whose strategic thrust is stable or reactive.

We label the coefficient of Figure 6.7 β_{ct}, where c denotes the level of competence and t the level of strategic thrust of the ESO. To simplify discussion, we have combined in β_{ct} both the general management and the logistic competence. In applications to practice, the two would be treated separately.

In the preceding section, we discussed the influence of capacity on the effectiveness of strategic thrust. We model this influence through the ratio $\frac{C}{B}$ where C is the capacity of the ESO, measured by the maximum amount of money it can effectively spend, and B is its strategic budget.

We recall that in Chapter 5 we related the effectiveness of strategic thrust of an ESO to the potential available in the environment, to the socio-political constraints, and to the critical mass. This relationship was:

$$ROI_{te} = ROI_{ee} \cdot \alpha_{te} \cdot P \cdot S \cdot R$$

ROI_{ee} is the maximum possible effectiveness of thrust e in environment e;

α_{te} is te ratio of the return available at thrust t to the return available at thrust e.;

ROI_{te} is the return on the investment for an ESO using thrust t in environment on turbulence level e.;

P is the political constraint coefficient in the environment;

S the critical mass coefficient in the environment;

R is a residual unexplained function.

In accordance with the above discussion we are now ready to express function R as:

$$R_{ct} = \beta_{ct} \cdot \frac{C}{B}$$

where:

R_{ct} is he applicability of the ESO's capability at level c to a thrust at level t.

When R_{ct} is substituted into the preceding equation, we obtain:

$$ROI_{tec} = \gamma.|ROI_{ee}|\cdot|\alpha_{te}|\cdot|P|\cdot|S|\cdot|\beta_{ct}|\cdot\frac{C}{B}$$

where:

$\gamma = 1$ when the signs of all of the terms which follow it are positive, and

$\gamma \quad -1$ when one or more of the terms is negative.

(For non-mathematical readers the vertical lines denote that we take magnitudes regardless of their sign, to obtain the product, and then make the product as positive or negative, according to the value of γ.)

The above expression is intended primarily to make visible the principal factors which determine the strategic potential of an ESO. We call attention to the change in the subscript which signals that the potential depends on thrust t, environment e and competence c. We would expect to make the formula more complex if it were to be used for computation of ROI_{tec}.

For readers who prefer verbal descriptions, the same results can be stated in terms of the following verbal hypotheses:

HYPOTHESIS 6.5: OPTIMAL THRUST

In each industry there is a strategic thrust which will produce optimal results.

HYPOTHESIS 6.6: LIMITS ON EFFECTIVENESS OF THRUST

In an industry for each strategic thrust there is a maximum attainable strategic potential.

HYPOTHESIS 6.7: MATCH OF THRUST AND CAPABILITY

For each strategic thrust there is a level of capability which will produce the most effective support.

HYPOTHESIS 6.8: STRATEGIC PERFORMANCE POTENTIAL

The potential economic effectiveness of an ESO in an environment is determined by a combination of the following factors:
1. The match between the environmental turbulence level and the strategic thrust;

2. The match between the strategic thrust and the strategic competence;
3. The size of the strategic budget (compared to the critical mass);
4. The strength of the socio-political constraints on the freedom of ESO behavior;
5. The adequacy of the capacity for effective spending of the strategic budget.

HYPOTHESIS 6.9: IRRATIONALITY OF ESO BEHAVIOR

A large percentage of ESOs do not choose the optimal thrust, nor support their thrust with optimal capability.

The above formula and the hypotheses shed light on the economic irrationality of ESO behavior. It will be recalled that the coefficient α_{te} is maximum at $t = e + 1$, when an ESO is an aggressive, but not a 'far out' leader in the industry. But relatively few ESOs in industry choose their strategic thrust at level $e + 1$. Thus the hypothesis of the economic theory, that firms seek to maximize their potential is denied. In place of this hypothesis we need to offer others which explain why and how ESOs choose their particular thrust. It will be our task to do so, starting with the following chapter.

7 Power

'War is too important a matter to be left to the generals.'

Clemenceau

EVOLUTION OF POWER STRUCTURE

We turn our attention from the effectiveness of a given strategic behavior to the manner in which that behavior is chosen. The choice is made by individuals and groups of individuals through a process which reflects their preferences. The choice depends both on what these preferences are and how they are brought to bear on the organization. We start with a discussion of this second aspect of strategic-behaviour: the use of power.

Definition: We define *power* as the ability of a group or an individual to affect any aspect of strategic behavior of an ESO.

Power affects the performance levels to which the ESO aspires, the behavior level it chooses, and the process by which it changes levels of behavior.

The role and the number of agents influencing ESO behavior has varied over the past hundred years. In the business firm the original all-determining controller was the general manager-owner. As firms grew and become more complex, management became separated from ownership. Owners held the shares and professional managers took over the management of the firm. Originally the managers did the bidding of the owners, but as the share owners became more numerous, more poorly informed, and less and less cohesive, top managers progressively acquired a controlling power over strategic behavior.

Continuing growth in size and complexity of the ESO and a changing social climate caused a progressive erosion of this power. Expanding cadres of middle and lower management, possessing their own expertise, and removed from immediate supervision by general management, became increasingly difficult to control. Experience increasingly showed that these managers were more highly motivated and more efficient when each was given a power domain over which he exercised complete authority and responsibility. As a result of these factors, power was increasingly decentralized to middle and lower management.

Meanwhile the shareholders were further removed from power. While maintaining the pious fiction that it works in the exclusive interests of the shareholders, management took virtual control over the fortunes of the firm. The influence of the shareholders was reasserted only when management failure brought on a survival crisis.

From the middle of this century on, the work-receivers, both blue and white collar, began to acquire power. For the white collar workers this occurred through accumulation of technical knowledge in the hands of non-management professionals, whose privileged know-how held the key to the ESOs success. In some large, technologically complex firms this accumulation of power led to a virtual takeover of power by the 'technocracy' and the middle management, reducing the influence of general management to a rubber-stamp ceremonial role.

The access to power by 'blue collar' work-receivers has been occurring on two levels: (1) at the work place, where workers increasingly participate in decisions over the conditions and content of work; and (2) at general management level, where workers act to protect and promote their interests during strategic decision making.

Dilution of management power has been a phenomenon common to both sides of the Atlantic. It is interesting, however, to observe the differences in the stimuli. In the United States the trend to worker participation was caused by a growing realization that 'a participating worker is a happy and an efficient worker.' Business firms sponsored research and experimentation with various ways of 'job enrichment', and introduced successful models at the work place.

In the United States the limitation on strategic power of general management has largely come from the outside in the form of legislation and social pressures to curb socially 'polluting' behavior. Most of these pressures have been addressed toward limiting and channelling strategic behavior (e.g. automotive safety and anti-pollution legislation). But, increasingly, voices are raised to demand restoration of stockholder power, increasing accountability and disclosure, and redefinition of the terms and conditions for the firm's existence in society (for example, through a revision of the corporate charter laws).

With significant exceptions, such as the 'Volvo experiment' in Sweden, the European worker participation has come through political pressures by unions and governments. The same pressures in Europe, rather than limiting the firm's strategic freedoms from the outside, as in the United States, have led to a direct involvement of non-managerial groups in the strategic decision process. The instruments used in different countries vary from nationalization of the firm, to public and worker representation on the board, to compulsory consultation laws.

Thus in a typical business firm today power is distributed among several constituencies: shareholders, outside political and social groups, general management, middle and lower management, blue collar and white collar work-receivers. This complexity of the power structure is approaching that of a typical non-profit, where general management has never been strong and technocracy has always been powerful. While the shareholders are missing in the non-profits, they are accountable to diverse citizens' boards, to subsidy-granting bodies and legitimizing agencies. In fact, the strategic behavior of most non-profits is determined either 'from below', or from outside the organization.

MODEL OF POWER DYNAMICS

In the upper right-hand part of Figure 7.1 we show, inside the oval, the strategic decisions affected by power and, outside the oval, the principal agents who exert power. For purposes of the model, we treat both white and blue collar workers as technocracy.

In the upper left-hand part we list the principal sources which give individuals and groups influence over others. The first two are usually possessed by external agents, who, through law or social pressure, influence the inside behavior. The third factor, resources and knowledge, applies to most agents, both inside and outside an ESO, who have legal or *de facto* control over resources necessary to the strategic work of the ESO. Factors 4 and 5, job-giving/witholding and rewards/punishments, are the traditional key source of managerial power, which is now being eroded by social contracts, guaranteed income, and job security.

Charisma, another traditional source of managerial power, is a personal attribute which enables certain individuals to convince the rest of the organization to shift behavior in new and untried directions. Such rare individuals exert influence through their skills of persuasion, ability to inspire others, and personal confidence-inspiring behavior.

The power to withhold effort is acquired when an individual becomes secure from loss of job and from punishment for malperformance. This type of power is more evident in non-profits, where job security and rewards and punishments are related to seniority and not to performance. Finally, the agents who control starting or stopping of organizational action can exercise important power over strategic activity even when they have no other power sources.

The exercise of power depends on its distribution among the various agents. At the bottom of Figure 7.1 we present three basic types of power distribution: autocratic, decentralised, and distributed, which span the range of observable power structures. Across the top we list the power groups, and the entries in the matrix describe the sources of power usually available to the respective power groups.

As the entries show, in an *autocratic structure* power is reserved for general management, except for the power of outside agencies to determine the ESOs terms of reference. Middle and lower management acquire a substantial share of power in the *decentralized structure*. Management as a class still retains the power of determining the strategic course of the ESO, but the technocracy has enough power to frustrate implementation of strategy by withholding specialized knowledge and effort.

In the *distributed power structure* technocracy acquires a deciding power over organizational work, and, when the ESO is large and complex, technocracy may dominate the strategic behavior. In distributed power structures control of job security and of rewards and punishments frequently passes to the environment, thus creating a fourth influential power center. The civil service, union seniority rules, wage legislation, and union contracts are examples.

In the United States a majority of firms today have de-

POWER SOURCES

CONTROL OF

1. Law
2. Society Norms
3. Resources/Knowledge
4. Job Giving/Withholding
5. Rewards/Punishments
6. Charisma
7. Withholding of Effort
8. Starting/Stopping Actions

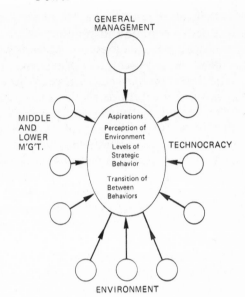

GENERAL
MANAGEMENT

MIDDLE
AND
LOWER
M'G'T.

Aspirations
Perception of
Environment
Levels of
Strategic
Behavior

TECHNOCRACY

Transition of
Between
Behaviors

ENVIRONMENT

POWER STRUCTURE \ POWER GROUPS	ENVIRONMENT	GENERAL MANAGEMENT	MIDDLE- LOWER MANAGEMENT	TECHNOCRACY
AUTOCRATIC	1, 2	3, 4, 5, 6, 8	—	—
DECENTRALIZED	1, 2	3, 4, 5, 6, 8	3, 4, 5, 8	3, 7
DISTRIBUTED	1, 2, 4, 5	3, 4, 5, 6, 8	3, 4, 5, 7, 8	3, 7, 8

Figure 7.1   Model of Power Structure

centralized structures, a minority have distributed ones. In Europe steps have already been taken in many countries to move the power structure toward the distributed power form. Whether this will happen in the United States is still an open question, although pressures for increased accountability of management, increased disclosures to the public, revival of stockholder power, and revision of the corporate charter laws all seem to be pointing in the same direction.

In the non-profits the instances of autocratic power occur in times of war and pursuit of urgent national priorities (e.g. the 'Sputnik crisis'). The predominant majority have either highly decentralized or distributed power structures (the former in cases of strong union power, or a strong coalition of professionals with a distinctive common ideology).

For describing the exercise of power within a power structure, we use three representative processes.

The first is *coercive* power process, in which the preferences of one dominant group determine the strategic choice.

The second is *consensual* choice of strategic actions. This typically occurs when several power centers share a common conception of organizational purpose – a common ideology – but have different perceptions of how this purpose is best achieved. For example, in a business firm, while all the major work functions (operations, marketing, research and development) share the belief in the common goal of profitability, each function seeks to influence the ESO into a different type of strategic behavior.

In consensual power processes, it is common to justify proposals for strategic actions advanced by the respective power centers on the basis of their contribution to the common good. In managerially sophisticated firms, it has become common to split the strategic choice process into two consecutive steps. The first is to specify the common purpose in the form of goals and objectives. The second step is to test the action proposals against the objectives. To the extent to which the testing is made explicit and quantifiable, the second step becomes a rational one and the power process is confined to the first step.

The third power process is one of *bargaining*. This occurs in situations in which there is more than one conception of the basic purpose of the ESO. For example, while top and middle managers in the business firm usually share the idea that the firm's central purpose is to make money, the work-receiving technocracy typically sees the purpose as maximizing both job security and the wages of the employees. In bargaining processes the respective aspirations of the power centers are not negotiable, because they stem from different ideologies. Negotiations are focused around action alternatives. The process is one of give and take in the search for an alternative which is acceptable to all interested parties. The degree of satisfaction obtained by each constituency is proportional to its relative power.

In Figure 7.2 we bring together structure and process. The upper left, doubly-cross-hatched box shows a typical situation in which groups or individuals possessing autocratic power prefer

POWER PROCESS ⟍ POWER STRUCTURE	COERCIVE	CONSENSUAL	BARGAINING
AUTOCRATIC (firms)	NORMAL CONDITION	FEASIBLE	FEASIBLE
DECENTRALIZED (firms, non-profits)	CRISIS CONDITION	NORMAL CONDITION	FEASIBLE
DISTRIBUTED (non-profits, future firms)	CRISIS CONDITION	INFEASIBLE	NORMAL CONDITION

Figure 7.2   Power Structure and Process

not to delegate it. The singly-hatched boxes in the same line show other alternatives which are feasible under the autocratic power structure but which are less frequently used. The middle, doubly-cross-hatched box is the historical situation in the firm in which management chooses not to admit technocracy to power. The right-hand, singly-hatched box, in the middle line shows the trend in firms in which professionalization of middle management, formation of management unions, and growing power of technocracy increasingly force bargaining behavior. Finally, the right-hand, doubly-hatched box represents a typical distributed power situation under normal conditions. As the figure shows, when ESOs are struck by a crisis, the behavior typically shifts to the autocratic mode.

Thus power structure limits the range of political processes. The process, in turn, limits the range of strategic behavior. In coercive behavior the alternatives admitted for consideration need to satisfy only one set of preferences held by the controlling power group. In consensual behavior preferences of several power groups are applied to the choice, thus limiting the range of acceptable alternatives. For example, in a firm dominated by the production department only the criterion of producibility (low production cost, using existing technology) needs to be met by proposals for new products. On the other hand, in a firm in which both marketing and production are powerful, the proposed products must be both producible and marketable. Coercive political behavior can be more rapid and decisive than consensual, because little time need be spent on consultations and negotiations.

In turn, consensual behavior is faster and provides room for a substantially wider range of alternatives than the bargaining behavior. In the latter, alternatives must meet the criteria of conflicting ideologies which substantially narrow the acceptable field of choice. Thus in the above example differences between marketing and production are a result of different interpretations of the best way to attain a common goal of profitability, whereas in a firm with 'worker power' the basic goals of the work-takers and work-givers are in direct conflict. The former prefer high labor content in the product in order to provide job security, while the latter seek minimal labor content in order to meet the goal of profitability.

The speed and decisiveness of strategic action are the lowest in bargaining processes, because of prolonged negotiations involving several conflicting power groups. Furthermore, the successive strategic actions may be logically inconsistent, as they reflect changes in power positions and results of 'quid pro quo' bargaining.

It is important to recognize that a particular power process limits but does not necessarily determine the aggressiveness of strategic behavior that will take place. An additional determinant is the quality of the *strategic leadership*, which we shall be discussing in detail later. A classical example of non-aggressive strategic leadership was that of Sewell Avery who wielded autocratic power over the Montgomery Ward Company. Mr Avery stubbornly refused to recognize the signs of basic change in the retailing business and adhered to the conservation strategy of maximizing the liquidity of his firm. As a result, Montgomery Ward came close to losing its position in the retail market.

The practical consequence of the progressive narrowing of alternatives, as one moves from coercive to bargaining behavior, is to reduce the potential boldness of strategic action. A coercive management group may not choose to be bold, but if it does, it can act more boldly and move more rapidly than management in a bargaining environment, where choice is forced to the least common denominator.

As mentioned in the introductory chapter, we treat power as an exogenous variable and do not generally concern ourselves with the mechanism by which a particular power configuration, is formed, or how power is transferred. However, there is one important situation in which strategic action and power transfer are closely coupled. This arises when an ESO is confronted with a survival crisis. In this situation the various power factions typically abandon pursuit of group interests and unite in a search for a survival solution.

This solution is typically sought in leadership. The prior leadership is discredited and power is withdrawn from it. The search is on for an individual or a group which promises salvation. If such a savior is not found within the organization, he is brought in from the outside and granted autocratic power to lead the ESO out of the crisis. As we shall be discussing, later, this act of voluntary political submission typically lasts only as long as a sense of crisis pervades the ESO. When the sense disappears, the various power centers begin to reassert themselves.

The above discussion can be summarized in terms of several hypotheses:

HYPOTHESIS 7.1: NATURE OF STRATEGIC CHOICE
Strategic choices are made through interaction of groups and individuals who have distinctive preferences and the power to support these preferences.

HYPOTHESIS 7.2: PROCESS OF STRATEGIC CHOICE
The mechanism of choice depends on a combination of the power structure and the differences in the preferences of power groups:

When power is concentrated in one group, the choice is likely to be based on its preferences only;

When power is decentralized throughout management, the choice is likely to be based on a balance of different interpretations of a common purpose of the enterprise;

When power is distributed between management and technocracy, or when management groups are ideologically polarized, the choice will likely be a bargain compromise which partially satisfies several conflicting criteria.

HYPOTHESIS 7.3: BOLDNESS OF CHOICE
The range of admissible strategic alternatives will be wider and the strategic process quicker and more decisive in a coercive power structure than in a decentralized power structure. Correspondingly, the range will be wider and the process quicker in a decentralized than in a distributed power structure.

HYPOTHESIS 7.4: POWER TRANSFER IN CRISIS
When confronted with a survival crisis ESOs tend to delegate power to a group perceived most capable of assuring survival, thus shifting to a temporary coercive power structure. This hypothesis follows directly from our earlier basic-survival hypothesis.

8 Aspirations and Culture

'You have to overpromise! The Sermon on the Mount was an overpromise! The Pledge of Allegiance is an overpromise! Anything worthwhile is an overpromise! What you *think* you can do is *half* what you ought to do!'

Hubert Humphrey

ASPIRATION BEHAVIOR

We turn attention from the dynamics of power to the motivations which affect strategic choice. According to our basic hypothesis, all ESOs are strongly motivated to survive. The less dependent an ESO is on its market and the more assured its subsidy, the lower will be the commercial performance needed to guarantee survival. A business firm which is totally dependent on the market has to maintain at least a break-even through commercial transactions. A university, on the other hand, which is heavily supported by income from endowment, alumni gifts, state grants, etc, typically operates at a continuous commercial deficit. Thus the basic survival drive induces higher performance aspirations in the firm than it does in non-profits.

Firms also differ from non-profits in the dimensions by which they measure their success. Some firms seek return on investment; others, return on sales; others, growth of sales; yet others, market share, etc. They do not necessarily confine their attention to a single aspect of performance. Some pursue one aim at a time but change aims periodically ('sequential attention to goals'). Others pursue multiple objectives simultaneously. Many firms, for example, pursue both growth and profitability at the same time.

Historically, all of the firm's aspirations were related to a basic drive for profit. In recent years, however, the changing social

107

environment has been forcing the firm to assume non-economic, 'social responsibility' aspirations, for fair treatment of employees, preserving of the environment, etc.

Non-profits have historically evidenced little visible interest in other aspirations other than survival. A minority of outstanding institutions has pursued a variety of objectives, such as prestige, excellence, rendering of public service, meeting a particular national goal (e.g. conquest of space). Sociologists who have focused their attention on non-profits usually describe the majority as non-aggressive, content to operate at a deficit, as long as it is covered by subsidies. Only when survival is threatened, do they turn attention to economic performance. Herbert Simon has labelled such ESOs *satisficers* and their level of deficit which triggers attention to performance as *survival threshold*.

On the other hand, microeconomists who focus on the firm seldom mention the survival drive, because they perceive the firm as a persistent maximizer of its economic performance. The model for this perception came from the early entrepreneur-owners who relentlessly pursued accumulation of personal wealth. After ownership was separated from management, economic theorists persisted in the assumption that professional managers continued the profit-maximizing tradition. Public pronouncements by managers reinforce this assumption. But empirical research and general observations show that today profit-maximizing firms are a minority of the total population.

Many firms exhibit *goal-seeking* behavior which stops short of maximization. They establish annual goals and adjust the vigor of their behavior proportionally to the gap between the goals and the actual accomplishment. Still others are satisficers, in the manner of the non-profits. Such firms differ from non-profits only in the fact that their threshold is higher. Because of their total market dependence, they turn attention to performance when profit turns into a deficit, whereas non-profits become concerned only when their deficit begins to exceed their subsidies.

The previous discussion shows two related measures of an ESOs motivations. First, the *dimension* of performance by which success is measured, and secon, the *level* of performance to which the ESO aspires. In normative business literature these two dimensions are called, respectively, *objectives*, (say, return on investment), and *goals* (say, maintenance of 5 per cent growth rate). Business literature asserts that when objectives and goals are made explicit in written form, the firm's performance is enhanced.

This does occur when the setting of objectives is followed by a vigorous control of subsequent performance. But some firms, following the fashion of the times, publicize their objectives in brochures and annual reports, but pay little attention to them in daily practice. On the other hand, the absence of explicit objectives does not necessarily imply the absence of a strong motivation to perform, as evidenced by many small, aggressive, profit-seeking firms, which do not bother to make their ambitions explicit.

Thus written objectives are not a sufficient measure for studying organizational motivation. This measure would exclude a majority of the non-profits, many strongly motivated firms, and would not necessarily measure motivation in firms with explicit objectives. To avoid these difficulties, we shall measure differences in aspirations in terms of differences in observable behavior. Organizations with explicit objectives will appear as a special case on a general scale of aspiration behavior.

Definition: We shall say that the behavior of an ESO is *strategically stable*, if the character of its linkages to the outside environment as well as its internal configuration remains unchanged.

A *strategic change* occurs when either the external linkages or the internal configuration or both change.

We shall say that behavior is *operationally stable* if the transactions through the external linkages are repetitive and routine.

Operating change occurs when the levels of the transactions vary, such as budgets, prices, and scheduling of output.

Complete operating and strategic stability describes a totally non-changing organization – a condition seldom observed in practice. To make the definitions useful we shall continue to call a behavior stable if the changes are occasional and do not consume a major amount of organizational energy. Thus, for example, we would describe a university as strategically stable if there were only infrequent and local changes in its curriculum. However, if the curriculum as a whole evolves continuously, even if incrementaly, over a period of time, we would characterize the process as gradual strategic change.

Definition: We define *operating* and *strategic aspiration levels*, respectively, as levels of performance below which an ESO is triggered into operating or strategic change.

The following are frequently observable aspiration behaviors:
1. Most non-profit ESOs are *satisficers* with a stable negative aspiration level. Internally there is no visible goal setting activity. Most of the time operations are routine and repetitive. Externally such ESOs remain, most of the time, both operationally and strategically stable.

The specific size of the deficit which triggers change is inversely related to the market dependence of an ESO.

ESOs with very low market dependence tend to be *crisis-prone*: their aspiration level is below the level of commercial performance needed for continued survival.

2. Some non-profits with high market dependence and a substantial number of mature, well-established firms (particularly firms in a near-monopolistic position), share a somewhat more aggressive behavior. They are *positive satisficers* operationally and *negative satisficers* strategically. A substantial performance drop below historically experienced profits from the environment will trigger operating counter-measures. But the performance has to turn into a deficit before the ESO starts making strategic changes.

The above two types of aspiration behavior are found in distributed power structures or in ESOs with very weak general management.

3. Many firms exhibit *goal-seeking* behavior in the operating mode and positive satisficing in the strategic mode. Internally there is an observable drive for continued improvement in performance. Objectives may or may not be explicit, but if they are, there is a strong discipline of assessing actual performance against the goals. By contrast to satisficing, which reacts after the fact, goal-seeking anticipates future performance and triggers change perceived necessary to meet the desired improvement in performance. Externally a goal-seeking ESO will be seen to engage in change a majority of the time. But it is not a compulsive, continuous change-seeker. Thus, externally observed, ESOs in

this category will be habitually engaged in operating change. But strategic change occurs infrequently, when it becomes evident that continued improvement cannot be achieved through operating changes alone. In such ESOs the most sophisticated mangement system is typically the MBO (Management by Objectives).

4. A typical American firm is found in the category of dual *goal seekers*, which pursue both operating and strategic goals. As we said before, objectives may or may not be explicit, but there is an observable internal drive not only to improve performance but also to improve and modernize the product/services the ESO offers to the environment. In sociological terms, such ESOs institutionalize innovation. If the objectives are made explicit, they are formulated through a participative 'bottom up' objective-setting process, usually within the framework of a long-range planning system. The power structure in categories (3) and (4) is characteristically decentralized, and general management is strong.

5. Finally, a relatively small number of firms falls into the classical microeconomic *maximizing* mode. They differ from the goal-seeking ESOs in the fact that the internal pressures are not for continuous steady improvement, but for extracting the last possible ounce of possible performance. Maximizers are compulsive change-seekers. Externally they are highly visible, because they are industry leaders in initiating both operating and strategic change. An example of their behavior has been vividly described by Edwin P. Land, the founder of the Polaroid Corporation: 'Our competition is our own sense of excellence. We are alone . . .because we plan ten times harder than anybody else and twice as hard as we do.' Typically, maximizers have an autocratic power structure and are coercively managed.

6. Normally, strategic maximization implies operating maximization. But there are significant exceptions of firms which are strategic maximizers and negative operating satisficers. They are exemplified by certain *conglomerate* firms in which management commits most of its energy to entrepreneural expansion through mergers and acquisitions and pays very little attention to assuring profitability of the acquired operations. Such conglomerates tend to collapse when management overexpands the firm while the operating results deteriorate into a bankruptcy.

The preceding six cases of aspiration behavior are illustrated, together with several others, in Figure 8.1 where the boxes representing the six cases are appropriately numbered.

The 'Industrial Leaders' in the lower right-hand corner are few in number, but they shape the course of economic progress. Around case (4) above we have illustrated the influence of the dominant function (finance, R & D, production, or marketing) on the aspirations of a firm.

Figure 8.1   Patterns of Aspiration Behavior

Strategic Aspirations	Operating Aspirations → Negative Satisficing	Positive Satisficing	Goal Seeking	Maximizing
Negative Satisficing	(1) Typical non-profits	(2) Low subsidy non-profits Conservative firms		
Positive Satisficing			(3) Production-oriented firms	
Goal Seeking		(4) 'Leading' non-profits* Marketing-oriented firms	Finance-oriented firms	
Maximizing	(6) 'Glamor' conglomerates**	R & D-dominated firms	Entrepreneurial firms	(5) Industry leaders

*Such as NASA, usually the nation's instruments for responding to a national emergency.
**Top management maximizes growth through acquisition, neglects operating performance.

By contrast to the scarcity in the lower right-hand corner, the upper left-hand corner is well populated with a majority of the non-profits. But non-profits whose subsidy is low and insecure are likely to be positive operating satisficers, sharing case (2) with 'conservative firms'. A non-profit which is a strategic goal seeker and operating satisficer is a rare but socially important instance of an ESO charged with an urgent and new national mission.

It can be seen from Figure 8.1 that the observable aspiration behaviors form a scale of aggressiveness of aspiration. The figure also shows that at the extremes of the scale the aspiration behavior of the firms and non-profits confirm to the stereotypes described in the literature. But between the extremes there is an overlap between firms and non-profits. As pressures on non-profits for a more effective performance continue to increase, we can expect the non-profits to shift toward the lower right-hand corner. On the other hand, as power becomes distributed in business firms, and as society continues to impose constraints on entrepreneurship and growth, an increasing number of firms will shift toward the upper left-hand corner.

Analysis, similar to the preceeding, could be applied to attributes of organizational aspirations other than economic effectiveness. If, for example, the attribute were *public service*, we would expect the pattern of Figure 8.1 to reverse, with many firms being negative satisficers and a few non-profits genuine leaders.

For future use, we summarize this section by means of the following hypotheses:

HYPOTHESIS 8.1: PERFORMANCE ASPIRATIONS
Over and above the survival drive, most ESOs exhibit a drive for economic performance above survival level. Non-profits typically exhibit satisficing behavior, firms goal-seeking behavior. Maximizing firms are a small percentage of the total population.

HYPOTHESIS 8.2: ASPIRATION BEHAVIOR AND OBJECTIVES
Aggressive aspiration behavior is not limited to ESOs which make their objectives explicit. Existence of explicit objectives, on the other hand, does not assure corresponding aspiration behavior, unless the performance is controlled to the objectives.

EVOLUTION AND INSTITUTIONALIZATION OF PERFORMANCE ASPIRATIONS

In their book, *The Behavioral Theory of the Firm*, Cyert and March open one of the chapters with the following provocative statement: 'People . . . have goals, collectives of people do not.'

Unless Cyert and March reserve the word 'goals' as a property of individuals, their statement is demonstrably untrue. Several thousand corporations around the world publish and use goals for the corporation as a whole.

When one reads Cyert and March closely, it becomes apparent that their provocative statement is intended to focus our attention on the fact that organizational goals can be traced back to goals of individuals. But it also becomes apparent that the goals of an ESO *cannot* be inferred *solely* from the individuals *currently* employed in the ESO.

To be sure, as Cyert and March show, current participants exert a major influence on the aspirations. We shall be discussing the reason and the mechanism of this influence in the next two chapters. But they also show that there are prior determinants which affect current aspirations.

At the time of its creation, an ESO is shaped by its founding fathers. They determine the products/services it shall make, the performance criteria by which it shall judge its success, and the performance levels it shall seek to achieve. In founding a business firm, entrepreneurs seek a return on their investment. Their aspirations are for high, if not maximum profit.

Non-profits are founded by a government agency, or a group of public-spirited individuals. The aim of the founders is typically to provide a socially needed service, such as health, education, or law and order, which cannot be met by profit-seeking institutions. Historically, founders of non-profits had little concern with economic effectiveness. The amount of money to be budgeted or raised was based on the estimate of 'what was necessary' to provide the service.

As an ESO grows and develops, two aspects of its founding aspirations tend to become institutionalized. The first is the *attribute* of performance, which is used to judge success or failure. In the firm the attribute is the measurable profitability; in non-profits it is usually a vague concept of 'public service.' In many non-profits, the economic attribute has what may be called a 'negative priority': it is not the positive, public-sevice contribution as much as a negative attitude toward economic effectiveness that is more clearly reflected in behavior.

The second aspect which is institutionalized is what we have called the *aggressiveness* of aspirations. As we have seen above, the non-profits persist in satisficing, most firms in goal-seeking or maximizing.

Part of the institutionalizing influences comes from the legal framework (charter) under which the ESO is founded. Another part comes from the prevailing social norms. For example, American society has historically put a high premium on creation of economic wealth. The firm was seen as the principal instrument of wealth creation, and profit a measure of its effectiveness. As a result, profit-seeking behavior was socially reinforced and rewarded. Successful businessmen were a privileged and prestigious social class. Aggressive wealth-seeking individuals were attracted to the business sector, while individuals with non-material aspirations and low risk propensities gravitated toward the not-for-profits, where they helped institutionalize the 'public service' aspirations.

The key attribute of performance is a stable aspect of aspirations. Once introduced by the founding fathers, it resists change. Thus, in all firms today the key attribute is still profitability, in spite of the many exhortations by outsiders that business should assume a broader 'social responsibility'. On the other hand, non-profits are strenuously resisting the concept of economic effectiveness. This was vividly illustrated in a recent article in the *Guardian* which complained that when the non-profits are under pressure to perform 'they either cut their services, or increase their prices'.

Agressiveness of aspiration is a less stable component of aspiration behavior. Initially while power is concentrated in the hands of owner-managers, the behavior of a new firm is likely to be maximizing. As the firm grows large and complex, power is increasingly shared, first with the middle and lower management, and eventually with the technostructure. In some firms top management skillfully controls the process of decentralization and preserves the maximizing orientation (a dramatic example: The Polaroid Company). In some other firms top management lets power slip away and becomes the technocracy-controlled, rubber-stamping stereotype described by John Kenneth Galbraith. As a result, the firm slips into satisficing behavior. To date, typical behavior of American firms has been between the two extremes. As the firm evolves, the original coercive power structure changes into a participative one and the aspiration behavior from maximizing to one of the varieties of goal-seeking shown in Figure 8.1.

In a preceding chapter we established that the type of power process used in an ESO determines the boldness of strategic choices. A part of that choice is the aggressiveness of aspirations. The relationship between the aggressiveness and the power process is illustrated in Figure 8.2. The figure shows the range of aspiration behaviors which are feasible under the respective power processes. At one extreme, under coercive power, all types of aggressiveness are feasible. At the other extreme, political bargaining inevitably results in satisficing. Within the feasible range the aggressiveness actually pursued depends on the strength of the strategic leadership – a matter we shall be discussing in the following chapter.

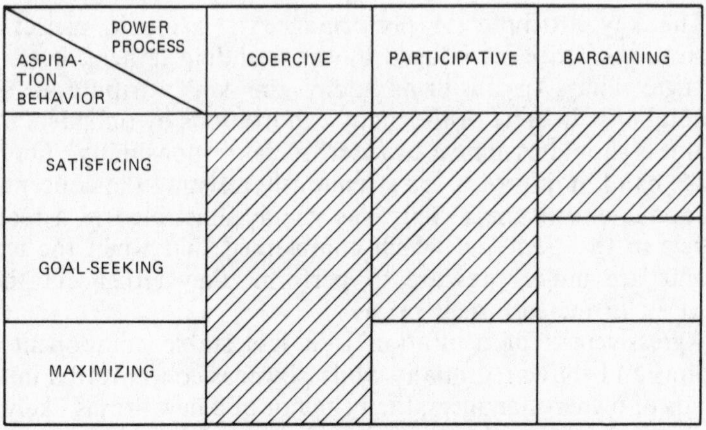

ASPIRA-TION BEHAVIOR \ POWER PROCESS	COERCIVE	PARTICIPATIVE	BARGAINING
SATISFICING	/////	/////	/////
GOAL-SEEKING	/////	/////	
MAXIMIZING	/////		

Figure 8.2   Range of Aspiration Behavior Feasible Under Different Power Process

Aspiration behavior is also influenced by the management system of an ESO (see Figure 6.2). The type of system used determines the attributes of behavior on which aspirations are built. Thus budgeting systems emphasize costs, management by objectives usually places emphasis on cooperation, organizational and self-improvement. Long-range planning directs attention to future cost-effectiveness: strategic planning, by contrast, pushes an ESO toward maximizing behavior.

The dynamics of systems' influence can work two ways. An established system tends to perpetuate the historical aspirations for which it has been designed. A newly introduced system, if it matches the historical aspirations, will also help perpetuate it. But if the system is at variance with history, it will serve as an impulse toward changing the aggressiveness.

In non-profits, separation of management from ownership occurs at the outset. Neither the founders nor the managers are preoccupied with performance aspirations. From the outset, general management lacks the coercive power of business managers. Power is distributed throughout the organization, thanks to local control over knowledge and resources, to job security, and to reward systems based on seniority. Thus, unless crisis strikes, a majority of non-profits start their life as satisficers and remain in this mode.

We summarize the preceding discussion in hypotheses:

HYPOTHESIS 8.3: STABILITY OF ASPIRATION BEHAVIOR

1. The *attributes* of aspirations inherited from the formative days of an ESO are the most enduring aspect of aspiration behavior.
2. The *aggressiveness* of behavior (satisficing vs goal-seeking vs maximization) is less enduring than the attributes. It changes during the process of organizational evolution, changes in key managers, and shifts in power distribution.
3. The *levels* of aspirations (thresholds or goals) are the most variable characteristic. These change as a function of the environmental conditions and ambitions of controlling power groups.

HYPOTHESIS 8.4: INERTIAL DYNAMICS OF ASPIRATIONS

The following factors act to perpetuate historical aspiration behavior:

1. Prior aspirations;
2. The legal framework of the ESO;
3. Societal perception of the ESO role and utility.

HYPOTHESIS 8.5: INFLUENCE OF MANAGEMENT SYSTEMS ON ASPIRATIONS

1. Established systems tend to perpetuate historical aspiration behavior.
2. New systems force a shift of aggressiveness and aspiration levels to become consistent with the system.

HYPOTHESIS 8.6: INFLUENCE OF POWER ON AGGRESSIVENESS OF ASPIRATIONS

The power process within the ESO limits the aggressiveness of aspirations:

1. Under a coercive process aspirations may range from maximizing to satisficing;
2. Under consensual process the aspirations may be either goal-seeking or satisficing;
3. Under a bargaining power process the aspirations will be satisficing.

CULTURE AND BEHAVIOR ASPIRATIONS

In the preceding discussion our attention was focused on the performance aspirations which may be called *teleological* goals, that is, goals which measure success by the results of organizational activity.

In the early prescriptive literature on strategic planning it was usually assumed that results were the only criterion by which success and failure of an ESO should be measured. Peter Drucker accurately described this assumption when he spoke of 'management by results'. The prescriptions suggested that the firm should choose the mode of strategic behavior (strategy) which led to the optimal results. If, as was the case in the early part of the twentieth century, the best profits were to be obtained by repetitive, routinized behavior, then the firm should choose a stable or a reactive strategic thrust. When in the 1950s success became dependent on anticipating or exploratory behavior, it was argued that strategic thrust should be changed accordingly. Thus strategic behavior was seen as *value-free* and as a means to the ends of profitable results.

Common observation and sociological research both show that behavior is not value-free, that both individuals and organizations exhibit preferences for certain types of strategic behavior. They express such preferences by persisting in a particular behavior, even if it means a sacrifice in the results. One common example is offered by older managers approaching retirement, who abandon their earlier drive for profit in favor of a safe and cautious behavior, an avoidance of 'rocking the boat'. At the other extreme are some corporate managers who push their firms into far-flung diversification primarily for the gambler's fun of 'playing chess with companies', rather than for enhancement of profitability.

Russel Ackoff was one of the first writers to call attention to the fact that strategic behavior is not value-free and that, just as firms aspire for results, so do they aspire to certain modes of behavior. Ackoff called these preferred behavior aspirations 'stylistic objectives'. Other observers have described them as 'organizational climate' or 'organizational style', or 'organizational culture'.

Definition: We shall refer to the norms and values of a social group which determine its preference for a particular type of strategic behavior as the *strategic culture of the group*.

In Figure 8.3 we have constructed six representative levels of strategic culture corresponding to the six strategic thrusts of Figure 5.9. This is to say that each of the states of culture of Figure 8.3, when left unconstrained, would exhibit a strategic thrust which bears the same name in Figure 5.9. The states of culture are described by six attributes, two of which are the attributes of organizational openness that we discussed in Chapter 6. The attributes are:

1. The *time perspective* in which the ESO perceives itself and its environment;
2. The *domain of alternatives* in which it searches for action possibilities;
3. The *focus* of organizational attention, whether inward on the internal events, or outward on the happenings in the environment;
4. *Change propensity* which is measured by the strength of the signal needed to trigger strategic change;

Figure 8.3 Strategic Culture

Level of culture Attribute	Stable	Reactive	Anticipating	Exploring	Creative
1. Time perspective	Past	Present	Familiar Future	Unfamiliar Futures	Novel Futures
2. Domain of Alternatives	Past Precedents	Past Experience	Extrapolated Possibilities	Global Possibilities	Creative Possibilities
3. Inside/outside Focus of Attention	Introverted	Introverted	Introverted/ Extroverted	Extroverted	Extroverted
4. Change Propensity- Strategy of Change Trigger	Crisis	Unsatisfactory Performance History	Anticipated Shortfall of Performance	Continuous Search for Change	Continuous Search for Novel Change
5. Acceptable Discontinuity of Change	None – Status Quo	Minimal Departure from Status Quo	Incremental	Discontinuous	Novel
6. Risk Propensity	Aversion to Risk	Minimum Risk	Familiar Risk	Risk/Gain Tradeoff	Preference for Unfamiliar Risk
7. Slogan	"Don't Rock the Boat"	"Roll with the Punches"	"Plan Ahead"	"Be Where the Action Is"	"Invent the Future"
8. Preferred Culture in:	Production Units Accounting Units	Production Units Financial Control	Marketing Units Planning Units	Product/Market Development Diversification Units	Research New Venture Units

5. The *discontinuity* from the past experience acceptable in action alternatives;
6. The *risk propensity* in the choice of alternatives.

The stable/reactive cultures are seen to be introverted, risk aversive, resistant to change. At the other extreme exploring creative cultures are open to new information, new influences; they welcome and seek change. The middle *anticipating* culture, which is found in many firms today, is change propensive, so long as strategic action is confined to the familar terrain.

In the seventh line we attempt to characterize the respective cultures by a single descriptive phrase, which may be used as an admonition given by old-timers to an ambitious newcomer to the organization.

Observed from the outside, most ESOs exhibit a consistent strategic thrust for long periods of time, alternating with periodic shifts in thrust. Thus an impression is created of a stable homogeneous culture on the inside. An internal observer will indeed find a homogeneous culture in a majority of non-profits and in what may be called 'single-function' firms, such as firms confined to research and development, wholesale distributors, etc. However, in multifunction firms, there are usually several distinctive cultures. This occurs because the technologies of the different functions demand different types of behavior. Thus stable and reactive cultures are best for manufacturing processes, for they offer advantages of scale, of division of work, and of amortizing organizational learning over long production runs. Anticipating and exploring behaviors are best for marketing, because they sensitize the firm to environmental trends, to customer needs, and to moves and counter-moves by competition. Thus we can say that each distinctive function has a preferred *strategic work culture*. In the last line of Figure 8.3, we have shown the match between the respective types of culture and different types of units in a typical manufacturing firm.

There is a tendency for each unit to regard its strategic work culture as the key to overall organizational success. As a result, they not only persist in their natural culture but also attempt to subvert other units to the same type of strategic behavior. Production units want the entire organization to be stable, marketing units want it to be anticipatory, etc.

Such self-centered perceptions of organizational success can be illustrated through the following historical anecdote. In the halcyon days of the aircraft industry a visitor to several offices of an airplane manufacturer was likely to find a succession of different cartoons pinned on a wall of the office. In the marketing office one would have found a picture of an airplane which is all fuselage – bulging with passengers – supported by two sticks, serving as wings, to which were attached two tiny engines. The propulsion office would have shown the same airplane as being all engines with structure only sufficient to support the power plant. Offices of other specialists would show similar biased perspectives.

Figure 8.3 can be used in two different ways: to identify the personal behavior preferences of key individuals, or to identify group preferences resulting from a common work culture. In both uses the preferences act on the ESO as aspirations: individuals and groups seek to influence the rest of the ESO in accordance with their preferences, judge their success by the extent to which they are attained, and will initiate change in strategic behavior in case of failure.

We can say, therefore, that in each ESO there are two different types of aspirations: *performance aspirations* for certain types of results and *behavior aspirations* for certain types of behavior. The success of the different units in imposing their behavioral aspiration on the ESO depends on their power. In performance-oriented ESOs this power accrues to units which are seen to be important to the ESOs success. It is for this reason that the production culture (called in business literature 'production mentality') dominated business firms during the 1900–40 period. After the 1940s, when marketing appeared to become the key to success, 'marketing mentality' began to replace the production mentality. This shift to the marketing dominance was slow and painful, accompanied by political struggle between production and marketing. The struggle occurred in part because production managers persisted in their perception that production orientation was the key to continued success. But it also reflected the strength of the behavioral preference aspirations by the production managers, who would retain stable/reactive strategic behavior *even if* it meant a lowering of profitability.

Gradually the shift to marketing mentality spread and marketing became the power center. In some firms the transfer occurred when power-hungry marketing managers overcame the 'tired' production manager. In others the change was triggered by the external authority of the board, which became concerned by an erosion of earnings. In a significant number of cases it took a survival crisis to wrest power from the entrenched production-oriented management.

Transition of power to marketing frequently produced an overswing. In the newly complex environment success was no longer to be gained through dominance of a particular work culture. Firms needed *both* enough stability to remain efficient producers and enough openness to change to respond to the environment. In such situations there was a gradual swing of the pendulum back toward the center. General management, instead of letting one functional culture dominate the behavior, developed an environment which enabled both production and marketing to operate together. This blend of the two cultures became known as 'the total marketing concept'.

Thus the external impression of a homogeneous internal culture may or may not be correct. The strategic culture is likely to be uniform and pervasive in ESOs whose internal work functions are technologically undifferentiated. This is likely to be true in not-for-profit ESOs, whose job is routine paper processing. But in a hospital, a university, or an integrated manufacturing firm, there are usually several distinctive work-determined strategic cultures (e.g. that of the doctors, the nurses, the administrators, the laboratory technicians). Each seeks to impress its behavioral aspirations on the rest of the ESO.

One result may be dominance of one culture over others; another may be development of a compromise dominant culture. A third possibility, frequently encountered in firms, is a multicultural coexistence, in which internal behavior of units is guided by their own work cultures, but the joint behavior is guided by a dominant culture of top management. The final and rare case occurs when there is no guiding dominant culture, but different cultures emerge as winners in the course of a continuous power struggle. The strategic thrust of such ESOs vacillates over time. This case is rare because such ESOs have a small chance of survival: they either go bankrupt in the market place, or are abandoned by their subsidy sources.

We can summarize the preceding discussion by means of several hypotheses:

HYPOTHESIS 8.7: DUALITY OF ASPIRATIONS
Individuals and groups typically have dual aspirations:
1. Performance aspirations for results of activity;
2. Behavior aspirations for a certain type of strategic thrust.

HYPOTHESIS 8.8: CULTURE AND BEHAVIOR ASPIRATIONS
Behavior aspirations are the results of norms and values which determine the strategic culture of a group or an individual.

HYPOTHESIS 8.9: WORK CULTURE
Organizational units with distinctive work technologies have distinctive strategic cultures.

HYPOTHESIS 8.10: MULTICULTURAL ESOs
The strategic thrust of multicultural ESOs either reflects the aspirations of the dominant culture or is the result of a compromise among several strong cultures.

9 Strategic Leadership

'Our competition is our own sense of excellence. We are alone . . .
because we plan . . . ten times harder than anybody else and twice
as hard as we do.'

Edwin P. Land

PATTERNS OF STRATEGIC LEADERSHIP

In an ESO the work-taking technocracy carries no formal
responsibility for the success and survival of the enterprise.
Nevertheless, as technocracy gains power, it exercises an increasing
influence on the strategic work of the enterprise. In smaller
firms workers frequently identify with the interests of the owner-
managers, but in both large firms and non-profits they increasingly
use their power to promote parochial, personal, and group
interests. As we have already discussed, the early influence was
over conditions of work at the work place. But increasingly,
technocracy, particularly the white collar specialists, has become
influential over the strategic activity.

Definition: We shall refer to influence on strategic behavior
exercised by representatives of special interests as *political
influence*.

In the business firm, the work-giving management *is* responsible
for the welfare of the enterprise. The very reason for its
existence is to provide guidance and control to the firm in a
manner which will assure its survival and success.

Definition: We shall refer to influence on strategic behavior
which contributes to success and survival of the ESO as
strategic leadership.

In the historical conception of the firm, the responsibility for

125

strategic leadership rested with two groups: the *shareholders*, who defined their expectations, and *general management*, which was seen as wholeheartedly committed to fulfilling these expectations. The shareholders expressed their wishes, general management interpreted these into appropriate strategic actions, technocracy carried out the actions under the guidance of management.

We have shown this historical perception in the upper left-hand part of Figure 9.1, where shaded squares indicate full-time and half-shaded squares part-time preoccupation of the involved groups. The political influence of the government was seen by management as periodic 'interference' in the workings of the free enterprise. The government saw its role as preserving the freedoms of competitive behavior.

As we have seen in earlier discussion, the pattern of influences today is significantly different. One new factor is a political influence by the technocracy, another is the increasing involvement of the government in determining the strategic course of the enterprise. A third is the political influence of the public.

Also, the behavior of general management is now seen in a different light. While there are still many totally committed managers, there are also many managers, particularly in the large ESOs, who use their office to advance their personal interests and ambitions, which are at variance and even contrary to the welfare of the shareholders. Even when they attend to strategic leadership, many managers are seen to be deficient performers, as evidenced by stagnant firms and firms in crisis. As we shall presently see, the failure to lead may be due to lack of personal motivation, aversion to risks, lack of requisite skills, lack of power.

In some firms strategic leadership comes not only from the general management group, but also from joint efforts of the functional management and technocracy. For example, the field salesman and development engineers, both members of the technocracy, may have a better perspective on the opportunities beneficial to the firm than does the general management. If general management happens to be weak, these technocrats, in coalition with their supervisors, may be the primary source of strategic leadership in the firm.

Thus the emerging pattern of influences is more complex than in the past. We demonstrated the new pattern in the upper right-hand side of Figure 9.1, which shows that strategic leadership is

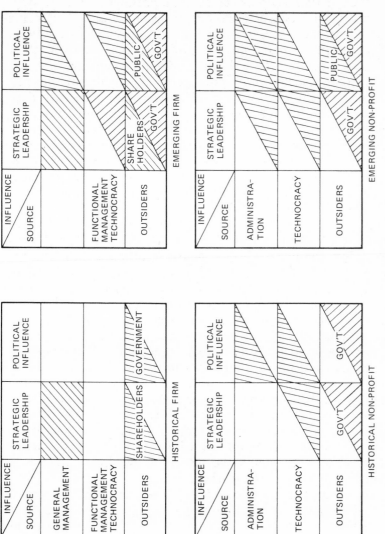

Figure 9.1   Changing Participation in Strategic Decision

no longer the exclusive privilege of general management. The figure also shows that strategic leadership increasingly competes with a variety of political influences.

Strategic leadership has been a rare phenomenon in the non-profits. On infrequent occasions, a visionary and charismatic individual set out to lead his university, or hospital, to a position of prominence, or an appointed leader (such as James Webb of NASA) guided a government ESO into a major strategic innovation (usually under pressure of an urgent national priority). Typically, creative leadership occurs during the early days of a non-profit. As it grows and matures it settles into the typical stable pattern, where strategic change is minimal, local, occasional, unguided, caused by external stimuli. Thus faculties introduce curriculum modification as faculty interests change; research gets redirected when new discoveries offer promise; medical care changes as new technology and knowledge become available.

In mature non-profits, the leadership for such incremental strategic evolution comes from the technocracy. There is no group, comparable to general management in the firm, which is formally responsible and accountable for strategic leadership. Management of non-profits is expected to stay away from strategic change – a domain reserved for the professionals. Deans are expected not to meddle in curriculum and research planning nor hospital managers in design of medical care. The job of the administrators is to assure smooth functioning of the organisation and to secure maximum possible subsidies.

A major reason for the strategic non-involvement of the managers in the non-profits can be traced back to the practice of setting up non-profits with a specific narrow strategic scope, and a low degree of market dependence (large subsidy dependence). As a result, the administration had neither the elbow-room nor the incentive to worry about the success of the organization, and about responding to the market needs.

The concept of strategic leadership has been absent from both the education and the culture of non-profits. The absence is underlined by a semantic distinction: in the firm the guidance and control function is called *management*, in the non-profits it is *administration*. When one examines the respective academic curricula, one finds that the education for strategic leadership is absent from schools of administration.

While strategic leadership is absent, political influence is rampant in the non-profits. It is made possible by the typical distributed power structure which provides a substitute outlet for the energy of technocrats and administrators whose jobs are not challenging, who lack a common purpose and a personal commitment to the success of the institution.

As discussed earlier, this situation is rapidly changing for many non-profits. Some non-profits need vigorous strategic leadership, because their historical role is being eroded, and they must either realign themselves with the environment or face extinction. Some others are being cast in the role of solving new societal problems whose strategic dimensions are poorly understood and which require creative strategic leadership (e.g. the new U. S. Energy Department). Many other non-profits are under increasing pressure to become more responsive to their clients, as well as to be more economically effective. One sign of the response to these needs has been the recent growth of interest by the non-profits in management education and particularly in techniques for strategic leadership, such as management by objective (MBO), and PPBS (planning-programming-budgeting). The emerging pattern of influence in such ESOs is illustrated in the lower right-hand side of Figure 9.1.

The key difference between political influence and strategic leadership is that the former calls primarily for exercise of political skills on behalf of a constitutency, while the latter, in addition to political skills, requires a clear perception of the common purposes of an organization and of ways to attain them. It is common to refer to such perceptions as the 'vision' of the organization's future.

In small firms such vision is often private to the owner-entrepreneur. But in large firms, to be effective, the vision must be shared by all those who are involved in its creative fulfillment. Thus the influence of strategic leadership is threefold: to conceive the vision, to communicate and inspire others with the vision, and to influence the firm to follow the vision.

But beyond influence, strategic leadership is also an intellectual task of giving concrete content to the vision in the form of common aspirations and strategic actions which can meet these aspirations. Thus we can say that the overall task of strategic management is to bring *organizational rationality* to the behavior of an ESO. We can sub-divide the total task into three subtasks:

legitimizing leadership, decision leadership and action leadership.

1. *Legitimizing leadership* involves establishing the purpose of the ESO and the criteria for its success. In the language of this book, this involves:

(i) identifying the key attributes (and their priorities) on which the success/failure is to be evaluated (the *raison d'être*);

(ii) identifying the aggressiveness of aspiration behavior (satisfying goal-seeking, maximizing) for each attribute;

(iii) determining the freedoms and limitations on the ESOs products and markets, as well as on its conduct (the rules of the game);

(iv) determining the power configuration which shall guide the ESO.

2. *Decision leadership* is concerned with making strategic choices. Specifically, this involves:

(i) establishing realistic levels of aspirations;

(ii) selecting suitable strategic thrusts;

(iii) selecting specific strategies and product-market moves.

3. *Action leadership* is concerned with causing the ESO to act in the selected strategic mode. Specifically:

(i) creating within the ESO a climate and capabilities supportive of strategic activity;

(ii) mobilizing management in strategic decision leadership;

(iii) influencing the work-takers to carry out the decisions;

(iv) coordinating and controlling the implementation work.

Definition: We shall say that the *degree of rationality* of strategic leadership is measured by the extent to which:

1. The aspirations established for the ESO fairly reflect aspirations of the influential constituencies which are affected by ESOs activity;

2. The actions selected are optimal for meeting the aspirations;

3. The actions selected are realistic in view of the conditions in the environment, the rules of the game and the resources available to the ESO.

Definition: We shall say that strategic leadership is *aggressive*, if general management exerts a strong influence on the ESO to behave rationally.

Definition: We shall say that strategic leadership is *successful* if the ESO meets its aspirations.

HYPOTHESIS 9.1
Strategic behavior of an ESO is determined by the competing forces of strategic leadership and political influence, both operating through the power structure.
Strategic leadership influences an ESO to behave in an organizationally rational manner.
Political influence represents parochial interests of power groups.

HYPOTHESIS 9.2
While strategic leadership is the nominal responsibility of general management, in today's ESOs other groups increasingly exercise strategic leadership.

HYPOTHESIS 9.3
Many general managers exercise weak strategic leadership. Many others use their office for exercise of political influence.

In the following sections, we explore briefly the observable practice in the three types of leadership.

LEGITIMIZING LEADERSHIP

An outstanding strategic business leader, Alfred P. Sloan, one-time Chairman of the General Motors Corporation, described his view of strategic leadership as follows:

> The strategic aim of an enterprise is to produce a satisfactory return on the resources invested in it, and if the return is not satisfactory, either the deficiency must be corrected or the resources allocated elsewhere.

Clearly implied in Sloan's remarks is the conviction that

aggressive pursuit of return on investment should be the basic aspiration of the firm. His view was shared by other business leaders, as well as by society as a whole. To Sloan and his contemporaries the need for legitimizing leadership did not arise. The centrality of the firm as the primary economic instrument of a society was obvious. There was a general agreement both inside and outside the business sector that the basic rule of the game was 'laissez-faire' – a freedom of the firm to pursue profit with a minimum of interference from the society. To be sure, the 'free enterprise' had to be protected occasionally from an overzealous government. But this was a low-priority task, typically delegated to staff public-relations departments.

In non-profits legitimacy was of even smaller concern. They were creatures of the government and the public. Their legitimacy was reaffirmed continuously through subsidy grants. The job of the administration was to perform the assigned public service.

As we discussed in Chapter 3, today the legitimacy of all important institutions is being challenged and re-examined. The issue of the proper roles for the firm, the university, the hospital, the Post Office is headline news, a major preoccupation of governments, and a challenge to managers in affected institutions.

This change is a symptom of the society's transition from the industrial into the post-industrial age. During some hundred years of the industrial age societal values and aspirations became clarified and stabilized, and various institutions evolved and settled into serving these values. One of the first consequences of the current rapid and drastic changes of societal values is to raise questions about the continued validity and the *raison d'être* of the existing institutions. When similar turbulent societal transitions occurred in the past, the result has been disappearance of some institutions, reshaping of others, and birth of new institutions designed to serve the new society.

A key question today is who will take the leadership in re-defining the role of the ESO. If history repeats itself, it will not be the managers inside these organizations. During prior similar social discontinuities (e.g. the fall of Rome, the Industrial Revolution) it was forces from outside the entrenched institutions that took the leadership. It seems that history is repeating itself. The major initiative for redefining the roles is coming from the government and the public. Thus in Europe the firm is being directed to assume social as well as economic responsibilities (e.g. maintenance of employment), and the power over strategic decisions is being distributed both to outsiders and to the inside technocracy. In the United States the government is shaping the product strategy of the automative industry, redefining the ethics of business behavior, and minimizing the pollution side-effects of business activity.

A majority of business managements has taken the position that society is in the process of destroying the goose that lays its golden eggs and that, sooner or later, society will come to its senses. According to this majority the role of management should be, on the one hand, to hasten the return to the senses by educating the public in the virtues of 'free enterprise', and, on the other hand, to resist all of the encroachments on business freedoms.

A substantial minority of managers has accepted the fact that the future is not reversible, and the firm will be changed from a purely economic to a socio-economic instrument of society. But this minority is still small and dispersed. To date it has failed to produce a coherent business viewpoint on how the firm can best continue to serve society. Experiments continue and the outcome is hard to predict. But the main point seems clear. Passively or proactively, management will be increasingly preoccupied with the problem of business legitimacy.

When this occurs, perceptions, attitudes and skills will be needed in strategic leadership which are not generally found in today's general managers. To deal constructively with problems of legitimacy, the leaders will need an understanding of the problems of society which goes beyond the limits of the business sector. They will also need an understanding, typical of all good politicians, of the ideological outlook of groups and individuals who will share power in determining the course of the ESO. Beyond understanding, they will need an attitude of ecumenical tolerance which respects the viewpoint of opposing ideologies. As a practitioner the strategic leader will need skills in the conduct of political processes: bargaining, conflict avoidance, conflict resolution. In brief, general managers cast in the role of legitimacy leadership will require the equipment of a statesman and of a politician.

HYPOTHESIS 9.4: SOURCE OF LEGITIMIZING LEADERSHIP

The initiative for defining the raison *d'être* and rules of the game for ESOs has historically come and continues to come from power centers outside the ESO.

HYPOTHESIS 9.5: IMPORTANCE OF LEGITIMACY LEADERSHIP

In the near future concern with the legitimacy of the firm will become a central preoccuption of general management.

DECISION LEADERSHIP

We have seen little historical interest by strategic leaders in legitimizing leadership. We now turn attention to strategic decision leadership which, it will be recalled, is a process of selecting strategic action thrusts for the ESO.

Because of their general lack of awareness of strategic leadership, little needs to be said about the non-profits. Their strategic actions are typically incremental and adaptive, determined by interactions of political influence and by shocks from the environment.

In the business sector as a whole, one finds that what it lacked in legitimizing leadership was more than made up by the aggressiveness of decision leadership. The rate growth, the proliferation of products and services, the relentless expansion of markets pursued by private enterprise have been truly impressive.

But within the whole, as we have already hinted in dealing with aspiration behavior, there are significant differences in the aggressiveness, the rationality, and the success of decision leadership. It has ranged from a minority of aggressive firms which invented and set the pace of progress, to a large majority which followed in the footsteps of the leaders, to another passive minority which resisted progress.

Creative decision leadership even in the large firms is frequently associated with a key charismatic, entrepreneurial, and forceful individual at the top of the firm. In the United States the names of Alfred P. Sloan of General Motors, Edwin P. Land of Polaroid, Pat Patterson of Texas Instruments, Henry Ford, the two Watsons of IBM, Donald Douglas of Douglas Aircraft and many others are associated with pioneering acts of technological and marketing progress.

At the break of the twentieth century strategic leadership typically came from top management. During the first half of the century, strategic leadership had been progressively decentralized out of the corporate office to the next one or two lower levels of general management. Each of these lower general managers had his own strategic domain for which he was fully 'profit-and-loss responsible'. A consequence of this change was a reduction in the size of the corporate office and in its concern with the strategic work of the firm.

From the 1950s firms progressively increased the number of their distinctive strategic domains. As the result of technology and the life-cycle phenomenon some strategic domains became saturated, others became strategically vulnerable, while others continued to show prospects for growth and profit. Thus continued independent pursuit of their respective domains by the divisional managers threatened to unbalance the firm and reduce the effectiveness of its resource employment.

As a result, a resumption of strategic leadership by the corporate office became evident in the late 1960s. This was not a recentralization of decision leadership, in the sense that the lower general management were deprived of their responsibility to exploit their domains. Rather, it was an assumption of responsibility by the corporate office for balancing firms as a total 'portfolio' of strategic domains. Top management began to assert its responsibility for strategic resource allocation among the domains, for adding new domains (diversifying), and subtracting (divesting) obsolete domains.

Assumption of strategic decision leadership by the corporate office will accelerate as firms become involved in legitimizing problems. This occurred recently, for example, in General Motors when it became evident that strategic behavior in all its divisions was going to be similarly affected by government regulations.

Today, there are several patterns of strategic decision leadership to be found in the business firm: (1) the case in which strategic leadership resides within general management, on levels below the corporate office; (2) the 'Galbraithean' case in which the technocracy is the strategic leader; and (3) the increasingly frequent case in which the corporate management manages the portfolio of the firm's strategic domains, and lower general managers are in charge of individual domains within the portfolio.

While, on the whole, decision leadership of the business sector has been aggressive and successful, the rationality of leadership has a mixed record. For one thing, many strategic leaders persist in basing the firm's aspirations on profit optimization, even in situations in which it is clear that values of other constituencies must be reflected in the aspirations.

For another thing, the choice of strategic actions on many occasions is suboptimal, as already discussed in Chapter 6. To some extent, this suboptimality is due to political influence, which deflects strategic leadership from its chosen course. To some extent, the cause is an 'informational irrationality' of the leadership itself, resulting from a distorted perception of the outside environment. (We shall deal with this important effect in a later section). To some extent, the cause is a 'cultural irrationality' – a persistance by managers in pursuing strategies familiar and congenial to them long after they become irrational for the firm. (We have already described this tendency in an earlier chapter.)

Such organizational irrationality frequently leads to *obsolescence of strategic leaders*. When managers refuse to respond to the changing condition, their strategic behavior become dysfunctional. Sooner or later such managers become responsible for loss of performance and failure, are discredited, and are replaced by others who are prepared to respond to the change.

The process of leadership obsolescence underlines the fact that the style of strategic leadership needed by a firm varies according to the environmental turbulence. This fact is contrary to a conception popularized in management literature, which holds up aggressive entrepreneurship as the single desirable ideal. As we have already discussed in Chapter 6 (see Figure 6.3), entrepreneurship is indeed appropriate to highly turbulent environments. But the entrepreneurial genius of an Edwin Land, the author of our chapter heading, would be out of place in today's steel, coal or petroleum industry. By contrast, the strategic conservatism of Henry Ford I was ideally matched to the needs of the automative industry during 1900–30.

There is another confusion between entrepreneurship and aggressiveness. It is popularly thought that the entrepreneurs are necessarily aggressive and reactive conservators are necessarily weak. While one would certainly not accuse General Motors of exhibiting excessive entrepreneurship, very few observers would deny a long tradition of aggressive, even if conservative, leadership.

Our final remarks are addressed to the role of systems and analytic problem-solving procedures in strategic decision leadership. Today, there is a curious paradox that while strategic decisions are the most complex and most important aspect of management, the process of strategic decision-making is the least systematized of all managerial decision processes. This does not mean that the decision process is not thoughtful and deliberate, but it does mean that in strategic decisions there is an inverse relationship between the complexity of the problems tackled and the amount of formal analysis that goes into its solution.

The reasons which explain this paradox are many. For one thing, many managers and academics still perceive strategic decision-making as an esoteric activity, whose essential creativity and vision are destroyed by attempts to systematize them. As a result, some observers recommend that in strategically turbulent times managers should abandon systems and return to 'plain managing', based on experience and intuition. Many managers, who never attempted to systematize their strategic thinking, gladly accept this advice.

Another reason is that, until as little as twenty years ago, strategic decision-making had a low priority. As a result, management systems and problem-solving procedures were tailored to serve non-strategic decisions and processes.

A third reason is that systematic strategic decision-making is alien to the prevalent stable, reactive, and even anticipatory cultures which adhere to past experience for predicting the future.

Finally, the technology of systematic strategic decision-making was invented only some twenty years ago and is still poorly developed. The part of the technology which deals with logical reasoning is reasonably advanced. What is missing are both the understanding and the technology of psycho-socio-political aspects of strategic decision leadership.

But with all these reservations, there are today more systematic inputs to strategic decision-making than is generally recognized. Capital budgeting procedures are standard in firms of any size, so are new venture planning, and acquisition analysis. Most firms active in R & D have adopted techniques and systems for project evaluation. Research and development budgeting is a part of the annual budgeting process. A growing number of firms relies on environmental surveillance for its decision-making. Long-range planning is widespread, and strategic planning is finally beginning to emerge after a ten-year gestation period.

It is not difficult to predict the future. Definitionally, intuition and experience become invalid when the problems confronting the firm are novel, unrelated to prior experience. Therefore, except temporarily, a retreat to 'plain managing' by the 'seat of the pants' is unlikely. More likely is an intensified search for creative managers with a natural talent for solving novel, complex, ill-structured problems. Increasingly, the talents of these managers will be developed and enhanced by new pedagogical techniques. Strategic systems will be used increasingly not to replace the new creative individuals, but rather to support them with essential strategic information and analyses of complex situations. Systems will also serve increasingly to relate multiple strategic leaders to one another.

HYPOTHESIS 9.6: RESUMPTION OF CORPORATE LEADERSHIP

A consequence of the present environmental turbulence is a progressive assumption of strategic decision leadership by top management.

HYPOTHESIS 9.7: MANAGEMENT OBSOLESCENCE

During transitions of environmental turbulence many general managers persist in strategic behavior which has become organizationally irrational. Such managers are eventually replaced.

HYPOTHESIS 9.8: STYLE OF LEADERSHIP

The style of strategic leadership which is appropriate to an ESOs success is determined by the environmental turbulence. In stable reactive environments entrepreneurial leadership can endanger the ESOs survival.

HYPOTHESIS 9.9: AGGRESSIVENESS OF LEADERSHIP

Aggressiveness and style of leadership are not necessarily

correlated. There are aggressive stable leaders and weak entrepreneurial leaders.

ACTION LEADERSHIP

A separation of decision and action leadership is somewhat artificial, because the two are the 'opposite sides of the same coin', not separable in either time or place. Many studies of decision processes point to the fact that a separation of leadership into 'planning' first, and 'implementation' afterwards, does not represent the strategic reality in which decisions and actions are interwoven in a complex sequential-feedback pattern.

But, for exposition purposes, the separation is useful because the two decision aspects call for different efforts from the strategic leader, and require distinctive skills and talents. Decision leadership requires marshalling of information, of intellectual abilities, of problem-solving skills, and of creativity toward developing strategic lines of action. Action leadership, on the other hand, requires marshalling of social energy and of motivation to *undertake the decision* activity, even though the consequences may appear unwelcome and threatening. Secondarily, action leadership requires marshalling the resolve to *carry out* the strategic decisions, even though the process results in unwelcome changes in behavior. Action leadership assures the will to solve difficult and unpleasant problems, and decision leadership assures that they are solved creatively.

Our preceding discussion shows that the need for both types of leadership is least when the strategic thrust is stable. The need increases progressively with the aggressiveness of the thrust. The greatest demand on both types of leadership is placed during changes in the level of thrust which are inimical to the dominant culture of the ESO. As we shall see below, the ability of leaders to lead in such situations is limited by the power they possess.

The combination of intellectual and social leadership skills needed for thrust transition is found only in outstanding individuals. Frequently, a strategic leader may have either the intellectual talent or the social charisma. Such duality results in several patterns of behavior. One is 'paralysis by analysis', in which plans are continuously made and remade by the visionary leaders, but little visible action follows. Another is 'strategic pragmatism', in which the strategic leaders are distrustful of analysis and imagination. This typically leads to incremental, 'muddling-through' strategic behavior. A third pattern is a version of management obsolescence described earlier. A visionary and creative leader expands the horizons and the fields of activity of the firm, but cannot marshal the social energy to convert the expansion into profit. Other leaders are brought in to replace him, to manage product and market development, to integrate acquired subsidiaries, to manage the new ventures.

HYPOTHESIS 9.10
Strategic leadership will increasingly require a combination of three archetypal behaviors: statesman-politician, visionary entrepreneur, charismatic 'doer'.

HYPOTHESIS 9.11
The greatest challenge to strategic leadership occurs in effecting a change in the culture of an ESO.

BEHAVIOR OF STRATEGIC MANAGERS

In the preceding sections, we have observed that while many managers boldly and forcefully influence the firm, many others exercise weak strategic leadership and some even abdicate their strategic responsibility.

There are several complementary explanations for such differences in behavior. One is due to the limitations on the power of general managers. As we discussed in the earlier chapter on power dynamics, the limits of general management power will vary with the power structure. An autocratic structure gives a manager the power to induce almost any change he may consider desirable. In a decentralized structure he must operate within the accepted ideology. He finds it relatively easy to induce changes which are culturally acceptable and difficult to induce changes which go against the cultural norms, such as, for example, a change in the level of strategic thrust or introduction of higher-level management systems. In distributed power settings with diverse ideologies a manager's influence is limited to changes in the aspiration levels and to incremental changes in products, markets, capability and capacity.

In each of the settings, when the manager attempts changes which exceed the limits of his authority, he is likely to be frustrated by the rest of the organization. In some cases, the organization may 'absorb' the proposed change in a welter of bureaucratic complications. In other cases, hostile power centres may coalesce to replace the manager.

Another limitation on leadership comes from the constraints placed on the strategic freedoms of ESOs by law, tradition, or social pressures. We have already ascribed the scarcity of strategic management in non-profits to the narrow strategic domains assigned to them.

Propensity to strategic leadership is also conditioned by the rewards attached to the manager's role. In many firms the financial rewards are related to the historical profit performance. As a result, in times of environmental turbulence managers in such firms refuse to take strategic risks, because such actions would entail near-term depression of profits. In non-profits rewards are typically unrelated to performance of any kind. Hence managers do not lead.

Personal strategic culture, ambitions, and risk propensities are another factor in determining leadership. It will be recalled that Figure 8.3 presents not only organizational but also personal cultural profiles. For example, personally 'stable' managers typically avoid and resist entrepreneurial behavior, partly because of personal and cultural preference, partly through fear of exposure, partly through a feeling of incompetence, partly through aversion to risk. Thus the rationality of a strategic leader's behavior is determined by the fit between his personal culture and the demands of the situation.

The aggressiveness of the manager's behavior will depend on his personal ambitions and aspirations. Some managers thrive on turbulence, others prefer an even, risk-free tempo of work. Some are strongly goal- and accomplishment-oriented, others are process-oriented, still others prefer a mix of 'the good life and money in the bank'.

When a manager is non-motivated to act as a strategic leader, or prevented from doing so, he may turn his energies to exercising political influence in order to promote his personal interests. The likelihood of his doing so is a function of the strength of his personal drives, as well as of the power and security of his position. Consider, for example, a manager in a not-for-profits, whose unit is a source of information that is vital to the functioning of the ESO, whose job is secure, thanks to his civil-service status, and whose salary depends only on seniority. Such a manager has the freedom to behave pretty much as he sees fit. By contrast, consider a business manager, who holds his job at the pleasure of his superior, whose salary is tied to his profit, and whose unit is not essential to the firm's success. Such manager has little freedom to deviate from the duties of his role.

The recognition of the importance of the match between a manager's personality and his assigned role is a newly emerging phenomenon. Many large business firms, which have been for a long time preoccupied with management development, have historically sought to mold their managers into a single cultural stereotype. Different firms developed different stereotypes. Thus a 'Shell man' was recognizably different from a 'General Electric man', or an 'IBM man', or a 'Unilever man'. But within each firm the same stereotype behavior was expected from everyone. To paraphrase Gertrude Stein, 'a manager was a manager was a manager'. He was expected to perform with equal skill and commitment in any leadership role which might be assigned to him. For example, a large U.S. firm saw nothing wrong in transferring the head of a refrigerator marketing division in the United States to the position of the presidency of a technologically sophisticated computer company in France.

Internally to the firm the enforcement of the single cultural mode has worked because, as experience has shown, a majority of individuals adapts to the culture of the organization and accepts its coloration. Part of the maverick minority moves to another firm. Another part of the mavericks stays on and seeks ways either to 'cop out of the system', or to make it serve personal ambitions, or to transform it.

Externally to the firm the single cultural mode also worked, because, as we have already discussed on several occasions, during the first half of the century success in the environment was possible through a monolithic cultural orientation. This was production orientation until the 1930s and marketing orientation thereafter. The respective cultures were dominant and the dominated cultures (such as R & D) contributed suboptimally, but without a major impact on the success of the firm.

Since the 1950s the success of the firm has become increasingly dependent on simultaneous contributions from a mix of leadership styles: stable conservator leadership, growth leadership, charismatic creative leadership, political statesmanship. As a result, it is safe to predict that, increasingly, ESOs will move from a single cultural stereotype to a *multi-manager* concept. Increasingly, the roles which general managers are expected to play will be differentiated according to the nature of the task and individuals will be selected, trained and promoted to serve in roles which make use of their distinctive personalities and personal aspirations. The above prediction is supported by the fact that the General Electric Company, which was a major contributor to the earlier concept of stereotype professional manager, has taken the leadership once more in introducing the multi-management concept.

HYPOTHESIS 9.12: POWER LIMITS IN STRATEGIC LEADERSHIP

In the absence of a survival crisis the magnitude of change which strategic leadership can introduce is limited by the power it possesses. When management attempts to exceed this limit, its leadership is rejected by the ESO.

HYPOTHESIS 9.13: RATIONALITY OF STRATEGIC LEADERSHIP

The rationality of the influence which leadership can impose on an ESO is limited by its power and the strategic constraints imposed from the outside.

HYPOTHESIS 9.14: AGGRESSIVENESS OF STRATEGIC LEADERSHIP

The aggressiveness of leadership is determined by the personal drives of the manager and the extent to which the rewards of his role meet his personal aspiration.

HYPOTHESIS 9.15: POLITICAL BEHAVIOR OF STRATEGIC LEADERS

Strategic leaders will engage in political influence behaviour in proportion to the following factors:
1. Their personal aggressiveness;
2. The dysfunction between role rewards and personal ambitions;
3. The power and security of their position.

HYPOTHESIS 9.16: TREND TO 'MULTI-MANAGEMENT'

In the future, the firm-wide stereotype of the 'company' manager will be replaced by roles designed to fit distinctive leadership requirements and distinctive personality profiles.

PERCEPTION OF THE ENVIRONMENT

Strategic leadership is concerned with tuning strategic behavior to the possibilities and threats posed by the environment. The quality of this tuning is limited by the quality of the information that goes into it. Therefore, a critical function of strategic management is scanning the environment for changes and trends and interpreting these into the performance potential available to the ESO. This is a complex process, based on both objective and subjective elements. The result is a managerial perception of the objective reality which exists in the environment, a set of beliefs of what is in store for the ESO. We shall call such beliefs 'performance expectations'.

Definition: By *performance expectations* we shall mean the performance which the management believes to be attainable by the ESO.

There are three sources of information which contribute to expectations. The first is the internally available performance history of the ESO, which by extrapolation can provide a forecast of the future potential. The second is the external environment, which provides indications on future departures from extrapolation. If such departures are unlikely, extrapolation will give an adequate view of the future performance possibilities. But when the departures are significant, formation of expectations calls for a third, internal source of information. These are the capabilities, capacities and resources of the ESO (frequently called 'strengths and weaknesses' in business literature) for coping with non-extrapolative aspects of the future environment.

The three types of information are processed in several steps. First, sources one and two can be used to produce an *environmental forecast* which identifies the potential available in the environment to a properly qualified ESO. Next, the qualifications of the particular ESO to capture a share of the potential can be estimated. This involves an analysis of the ESOs capabilities (strengths and weaknesses analysis). Thirdly, strengths and weaknesses are applied to the environmental forecast to obtain the *ESOs forecast* (in the firm usually called a *sales forecast*).

In a majority of not-for-profits and in most small firms the forecasting process is informal. Neither the sequence nor the interaction among the various elements is made explicit. A manager observes, estimates and judges at the same time.

The key element in the accuracy of the results is the manager's strategic culture, which determines both the time perspective in which he views the environment and the scope of alternatives which he accepts as credible. If the time perspective matches or exceeds the time horizon demanded by the speed of environmental change, and if the scanned events cover the range of probable discontinuities in the environment, the manager's expectations will be an accurate reflection of the probable course of the environment. But if the time and action perspectives are narrower than the environment, important future events will be excluded and some events will be perceived too late for a timely reaction. As a result, the expectation will be inaccurate and unrealistic.

> *Definition*: We shall say that an ESO is *myopic* if its perception of the environment is narrower than needed to capture the full scope of the environmental turbulence.
> We shall say that it is *in tune* with the environment when the range of its perception matches the environmental turbulence.
> We shall say that an ESO is *foresightful* when its perception scope exceeds that of the current environmental turbulence.

An ESO which is myopic will have inaccurate performance expectations. The expectations of an ESO in tune with the environment will be potentially accurate (subject to the quality of forecasting technology to be discussed below), so long as the level of environmental turbulence remains stable. But a 'tuned-in' ESO quickly falls out of tune when the level of environmental turbulence shifts. This occurs when, after a long period of stable turbulence, the turbulence level rises or falls to a new level. During, and for a substantial period after the change, a majority of ESOs typically remain myopic with respect to the new level of turbulence. An example of this was offered recently by the tardy and belated recognition by the U.S. automotive industry of the importance, and the impact of the entry of the U.S. Government into regulation, of automatic performance.

The advantage of a foresightful perception is twofold: (a) it enables an ESO to anticipate shifts in environmental turbulence and thus avoid strategic surprises; and (b) it enables an ESO to anticipate and to react to threats and opportunities ahead of other ESOs in the industry. But foresightful ESOs are a minority of the total population.

When the expectations are arrived at informally, factors other than culture contribute to their inaccuracy. One of these is the limited power of unaided observation, another is the limitations of intuition and experience. In stable/reactive environments intuition and experience serve well. But they become inadequate in anticipatory environments and misleading in exploring/creative ones.

Recognizing these limitations, many medium and large-sized firms increasingly use formal scanning and forecasting. Environmental surveys are prepared by staffs and submitted to decision-makers, who examine and modify the forecasts for accuracy and 'realism' and publish the result as the official expectations to be used by the firm. The formal process is both explicit and sequential. First, staff forecasts are prepared; next these are converted into management's forecasts. Both are prepared in written form and disseminated to the relevant decision centres.

Formal forecasting is subject to the same inherent limitations as the informal process. One of these, which we shall call a *forecasting filter*, comes from the methodology used in making forecasts. A reference back to Figure 6.2 recalls that ESOs in different states of competence use different environmental scanning and forecasting technologies. In the stable competence reliance is placed on past experience and no formal scanning or forecasting is made. Reactive competence formally extrapolates past costs (through budgeting). Anticipating competence adds formal performance extrapolation (through sales forecasting). All three approaches are based on the assumption that the future trends will be a smooth extension of the past. All three will fail to capture significant changes in trends, as well as possible sudden discontinuities.

As Figure 6.2 shows, the inquiring/creative competences use

techniques which forecast probable deviations from past patterns. Among these are the Delphi technique, impact analysis, scenarios, morphological maps, environmental modelling, etc. But different techniques capture different aspects of the potential future. Some, such as morphological maps and modelling, deal with shifts in the trends, while others, such as Delphi or impact analysis, try to capture singular events which may upset the trends.

Thus the technology used for forecasting interposes a filter between management and the environment. A myopic forecasting filter, which is narrower than the environmental turbulence, will present inaccurate forecasts to the management. A tuned filter will accurately reflect the environment, provided the turbulence level is stable. A foresightful filter will anticipate changes in turbulence.

The second type of filter is applied by the cultural perspective of the decision-makers. If this cultural *perception filter* is narrower than the forecasting filter, management will further restrict the perception of the environment by rejecting as inaccurate or irrelevant, information which is inconsistent with its past experience. A dramatic example of such rejection was the recent 'petroleum crisis'. In the aftermath of the crisis, it became clear that accurate and detailed forecasts of the actions by the Arab countries had been available to many of the firms which were 'surprised'. But prior to the actual event, these forecasts were treated as improbable or irrelevant and remained unheeded by the management.

HYPOTHESIS 9.17: ORGANIZATIONAL MYOPIA
During changes in environmental turbulence ESOs typically become myopic. As a result, their response lags the events in the environment.

HYPOTHESIS 9.18: FILTERED PERFORMANCE
EXPECTATIONS
The accuracy of an ESOs performance expectations is limited either by the forecasting or the perception filter, whichever is the narrower. When the narrower filter excludes important environmental trends and probable events, the performance expectations of the ESO will be inaccurate regardless of the computational refinement of the forecasting methodology.

COMMUNICATION OF EXPECTATIONS

Knowledge and awareness of expectations, whatever their quality, is typically confined to a small percentage of an ESOs
participants. In the firm the best informed and concerned are the
general managers who are responsible for strategic decisions;
managers in 'interface functions' (e.g. marketing, public relations, industrial relations, research and development) who
are in continuous contact with the environment are the next
best informed about expectations. But the very much larger
group of introverted managers and technocrats concerned
with internal operations of the ESO, usually have little
concern for and, frequently, little knowledge of what is in store
for the ESO.

In the non-profits there is usually no formal communication
system. Communications are informal, anecdotal, and confined
to interacting levels of the ESO. As a result, when the responsible
administrators become aware of a danger to the survival of the
ESO, a *communication gap* develops between them and the rest of
the organization. As we have already discussed, when confronted
with a crisis, ESOs suppress parochial political-influence behavior and support strategic leaders who promise salvation. But
this does not begin to happen until a general awareness of a crisis
permeates the organization.

The closing of the communication gap involves not only
disseminating the information about the impending crisis, but
also convincing the recipients that the information is valid. The
process is a delicate one, because on the one hand a brutal
disclosure of the full nature of the danger can cause a panic; and
on the other hand a cautious disclosure by the top administrators
may carry little persuasion and weight. This occurs particularly in
cases in which prior behavior of the administration has been
political, devoid of strategic leadership. When such administrators suddenly signal grave difficulties, they are likely to be
suspected of doing so in order to gain control over the organization, or to pass the blame to others. As a result, after the
responsible administrators become convinced of an impending
crisis, there is a substantial time period during which their
expectations are not shared by others, who continue 'business as
usual'. Frequently, it takes unambiguous signs of an actual crisis to

bring about a closing of the ranks in a common perception of the problem.

Business firms, particularly medium and large-sized ones, typically have established formal communication systems (See lines (d), (f), (g) of Figure 6.2). But curiously enough, in a majority of firms today, the communication system is a dual one. On all levels of capability of Figure 6.2, there is usually a performance-based communications system which reports past performance results on a periodic basis throughout the year. These results are widely disseminated to all levels of management. In firms with anticipating, inquiring and creative capabilities there is a second system for disseminating the results of the forecasting efforts described in the preceding sections. The forecasts are typically communicated through channels which are different from the performance communications and are confined to individuals responsible for the planning process. The forecasting information is typically disseminated on an annual basis in preparation for the annual periodic cycle.

The chances of important strategic information being communicated to the organization are thus very much higher in the firm than in a non-profit. But the business systems have their own deficiencies. One of these is the limitation of forecasting data to annual communications, which delays organizational awareness of key changes which occur in between the planning cycles. Another, as we discussed in Chapter 4, is the limitation of information to 'strong signals', which deprives the firm of an early warning of fast developing changes.

A third deficiency results from the duality of the communication systems on the one hand, and from the limited distribution of the expectations on the other. A large percentage of individuals who become involved in a strategic shift normally see only historical performance results. When a situation arises which calls for a fundamental strategic reorientation, top management typically communicates within the established expectations-communications system, leaving out the much larger population which will be affected by the reorientation. Frequently, the start of triggering a strategic shift takes this large population by surprise.

In cases when management attempts to communicate to all those concerned in advance of the shift, people accustomed to dealing only with historical performance results have difficulty in understanding and interpreting the new information. In either case, a communication gap develops which reinforces the inertial resistance to change.

HYPOTHESIS 9.19: EXPECTATIONS-COMMUNICATIONS GAP

When, as a result of a change in turbulence, the expectations of the general management of an ESO change suddenly, the perception of these expectations by other participants lags behind. The duration of the lag is inversely related to the quality of the strategic information system within the ESO.

10 Model of Strategic Choice

'Nous devons attendre que chaque trait d'une culture qu'on examine ne soit pas simplement économique, religieux ou structural, mais qu'il participe de tous ces attributs, selon le point de vue sous lequel nous le regardons.'

Gregory Bateson

'Man-evolved decision-making paradigms must be amplified rather than replaced, understood rather than ignored, respected rather than degraded.'

Milan Zeleny

As we have done earlier in the book, we follow an exploratory discussion with an attempt to bring together the several determinants of strategic choice.

In order to perceive 'the wood defined by the trees', we use schematic decision flow charts which provide a concise picture of the major relationship and interactions. However, readers who are not trained in formal logic and use of flow charts may find the reasoning difficult to follow. For such readers, we provide in the following section a verbal summary of the principal forces and influences which affect strategic choice and strategic behavior.

ACTION POTENTIAL AND INFLUENCE POTENTIAL

In the preceding chapters, we have explored a number of key forces and influences which determine the strategic behavior of an ESO. In the following chapters we shall begin to put these forces together to describe two aspects of behavior: (1) the manner in which the forces combine to produce strategic choices, specifically:

the perception of the environment, the choice of aspirations, the choice of the strategic thrust; and (2) the manner in which the forces interact during the transition from one strategic mode to another.

We can subdivide the principal forces and influences on strategic behavior into two groups. The first are more properly called influences, rather than forces, because they exert a passive, even if influential effect on strategic activity. These are:

The strategic culture which, we recall, is the strategic action propensity. In a given organizational unit this propensity is usually for a particular type of strategic thrust. When an ESO is engaged in this type of thrust, the culture will act as a supportive influence. When the behavior is in a contrasting mode, the culture will act to resist and frustrate the thrust, the resistance being proportional to the difference between the preferred and the imposed thrust. In a following chapter we shall model this cultural influence as the *cultural component of social* inertia.

The next two influences can be discussed together because they have a similar effect on strategic action. They are, respectively, the management and the logistic competence. When the level of thrust and the level of competence are matched an optimal outcome will result.

As the gap between the competence and the thrust increases, the effectiveness of the results will continue to drop. At an extreme, when the gap is large, the competence becomes a deterrent to the thrust and will actually produce negative results. Thus, for example, an attempt to force a firm with a stable competence into a creative behavior is certain to produce a non-profitable result.

The logistic and the managerial competence affect not only the outcome, but also the choice of strategic behavior. When traditional systems, structures and procedures are entrenched in an ESO, they create an inertial dynamic which resists and frustrates strategic thrusts which are not consonant with the competence. In sociological literature this type of influence is referred to as the force of tradition, which tends to perpetuate historical behavior. We shall be modelling this as the *systemic component of social inertia.*

Finally, the capacity of the organization affects strategic action in a fairly obvious way by introducing queueing and time delays when the capacity is inadequate for handling the strategic budget chosen by the ESO.

All of these influences are seen to play a passive rather than an active role in strategic behavior. They do not trigger strategic action, but they affect both its course and outcomes in a significant (positive or negative) way.

Definition: We shall refer to the set of influences which affect the outcome and the course of strategic action as the *strategic action* potential.

There is another set of what may be properly called *forces* which do trigger strategic action and which do affect the choice of the strategic action. These are:

1. The performance aspirations of individuals or groups;
2. The cultural aspirations which affect the choice of the strategic thrust. Thus culture can be seen to play both an active and a passive role. The extent to which it plays an active role depends on the following three forces:
   a. the achievement drive of key individuals and groups.
   b. the power structure which determines the ability of various individuals to impress their aspirations on others;
   c. the strategic management. The influence of strategic management toward what we have called organizationally rational behavior depends on the role structure, the rewards, and the power assigned to the individuals who occupy strategic leadership roles.

Definition: We shall refer to the set of forces which affect the initiation and choice of strategic action as the *strategic influence potential.*

In summary, the strategic influence potential starts strategic change and selects its goals and modalities, whereas strategic action potential affects the course and the outcomes of the choices. We next turn to a somewhat more structured examination of how the two potentials interact.

MODEL OF PERFORMANCE EXPECTATIONS

Information about future possibilities comes from the environment and from previous history. For the latter an ESO has access to its own historical performance, as well as that of its competitors. In the firm, for example, it is the history of sales, earnings, market shares, return of sales, earnings, market shares, return on investment, etc. Secondly, an ESO can describe its past in terms of the events and forces which were instrumental in determining the past performance – for example, growth in gross national product, structure of the markets, technological change, competitive behavior, etc. Thirdly, an ESO can describe its past in terms of the capabilities and capacities it has developed over time.

As discussed in Chapter 5, the historical information can be synthesized along two key dimensions: predictability of events and their degree of discontinuity from preceding experience.

Together, the two dimensions describe the turbulence of the historical environment. We shall represent the historical turbulence by a set of events $\{A\}_H$. The subscript H designates the level of turbulece which has prevailed in the past. Thus $H = 1$ would represent the stable turbulence level, $H = 2$, the reactive, etc.

In addition to historical events, an ESO can observe the *patterns of change*: the change in the relative importance of the historical events and trends, new events and trends which are emerging, new relationships among the forces which will determine the performance possibilities in the future.

We model the pattern of change by a set $\{A\}_T$ in which the subscript T denotes the level of the probable future turbulence in the environment, say, a shift from the historical anticipatory environment ($H=3$) to an exploring environment ($T=4$).

The sets are illustrated in Figure 10.1, in which environmental events and forces are characterized by two dimensions: the first, shown vertically, is the predictability (which, it will be recalled from Chapter 5, is the state of knowledge at which ESOs must start their response). The second dimension, shown horizontally, is the degree of discontinuity (measured by a combination of novelty and frequency) of the respective events from the past. The two free-form shapes are the boundaries of sets $\{A\}_H$ and $\{A\}_T$.

A comparison of the two sets shows the future turbulence to be considerably greater than the past: many new events will occur,

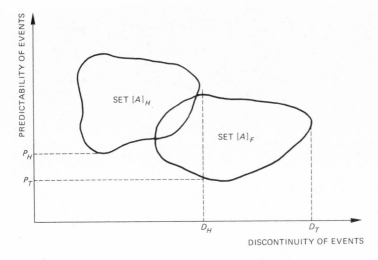

Figure 10.1   Map of Past and Future Turbulence

they will impact faster, and at the same time will be more discontinuous from the past. This gives a strong indication that future performance possibilities will be significantly different from, and determined by different factors than in the past.

A simple, if incomplete way to characterize the impending shifts in turbulence is by the coordinates of the extreme events in each set. Thus the set (P_H, D_H) has higher predictability of impact and lower maximum degree of discontinuity than the set (P_T, D_T).

In Figure 10.2 we model the different ways in which information is acquired by an ESO and translated into expectations about the future. Following the preceding discussion, we subdivide the information sources into *historical environment*, characterized by the level of turbulence *H*, and the *future environment* characterized by *T*.

As the figure shows, some ESOs neither record their history nor scan their environment. These are typically satisficers, whose threshold is a crisis. They are closed to all environmental influences, except for an imminent survival threat. Their existence is a day-to-day coping with yesterday's problems. Members of such ESOs have no shared expectations about the future.

Another significant, and probably the largest, class of ESOs does not scan the environment but has a sense of history, thanks

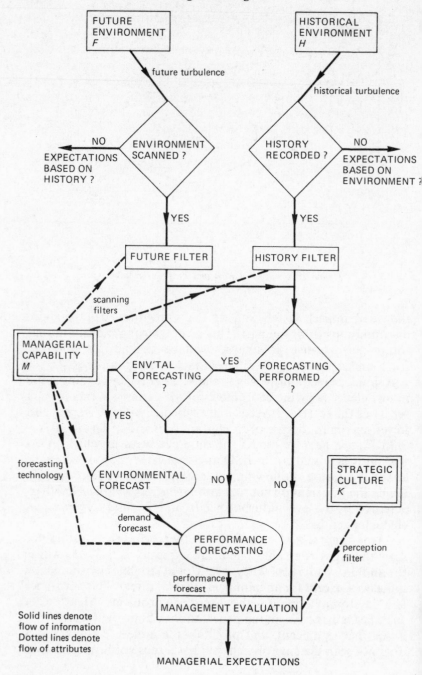

either to written records of past performance, or to memories shared by the managers.

A third class of ESOs, usually business firms, is aware of both history and the surrounding environemnt. The numerous past events and transactions within such ESOs are usually recorded by the accounting system. Environmental scanning can range from a personal informal contact with the immediate environment to sophisticated systems which attempt to identify significant signals beyond the immediate perceptions of the managers.

But usually only a part of the available information is admitted into the ESO for subsequent processing. As Figure 10.2 shows, both the prospective future and the history are filtered through *scanning filters*. In ESOs which have no formal management information systems, the filters are the personal limitations of the manager's skills to observe and interpret data. In ESOs with formal systems the characteristics of the filter are determined by the technology of the system.

If the manager's or the system's ability to observe is more limited and narrower than the scope of turbulence in the environment, the scanning filter will exclude important future possibilities. As a result, the ESOs picture of the external reality will be incomplete and inaccurate. This is illustrated in Figure 10.3, where the dotted line labelled 'scanning filter' shows how a restrictive filter can exclude a part of the historical record, as well as most of the future possibilities. (We shall be discussing presently the other filters shown in Figure 10.3.)

Returning to Figure 10.2, we show that further processing of the scanned information can follow one of several paths. If an ESO has no formal forecasting procedures, the information goes directly to the decision-maker, who in this case very probably is also the scanner.

The decision-maker will use the information to form his personal expectations about the possible future of the ESO. In doing this he will judge the validity and the reliability of the scanned data and thus apply to it a *perception filter*. The limits of this filter will be set by the manager's personal strategic culture, personality, and prior experiences.

An alternative path for the scanned information is to provide an input into formal and explicit estimates, *forecasts* of the future. As Figure 10.2 shows, a further branching of the process depends on whether the ESO performs both environmental and performance

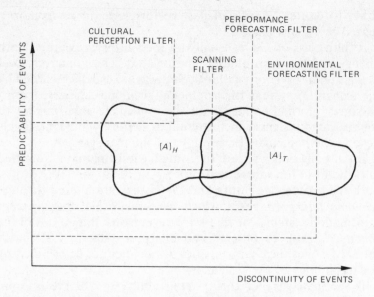

Figure 10.3   Effect of Strategic culture and Management Capability on perception of Turbulence

forecasting, or only performance forecasting.

Until some fifteen years ago, organized forecasting was to be found primarily in medium and large business firms, and a majority of these confined themselves to performance forecasting. As we discussed earlier, in the absence of environmental forecasting, performance forecasting involves extrapolation of history. Returning to Figure 10.3, we see that extrapolative performance forecasting introduces another filter by limiting the data used to set $\{A\}_H$ and excluding most parts of $\{A\}_T$ which do not overlap with $\{A\}_H$. In Figure 10.3, the cultural filter determines the richness of the information used by management. The figure illustrates the case in which the scanning input to the forecasts limits their accuracy and in which the perception filter is the ultimate limiting factor in performance expectations. This is a case in which the system is too sophisticated for the management.

As we have discussed previously, some fifteen years ago the decreasing predictability of the environment made extrapolative forecasting increasingly inadequate. Firms reacted with a growing interest in environmental forecasting.

As discussed earlier, an environmental forecast uses both historical and future turbulence to convert scanned signals into the future potential demand. This potential demand provides a more reliable basis for performance forecasting than a direct extrapolation of the past. But again, if the environmental forecasting technique used is not powerful enough to handle the full range of discontinuity of the set $\{A\}_T$, it will keep the ESO from perceiving the full richness of the environment. If, for example, the technique is a 'smoothing' one, it will predict smooth trends in the environment which, in fact, may have substantial discontinuities. Or the model (such as Delphi) may focus on the impact of singular events, but will have nothing to say about important changes in the secular trends.

Thus although environmental forecasting enriches and improves performance forecasting, if its scope does not match the environmental turbulence, it will fail to give ESOs a complete perspective on the environment. This is illustrated in Figure 10.3 by the *environmental-forecasting filter*.

Thus before the input information reaches the decision-maker, it is subject to three filters. These are the scanning filter, the environmental-forecasting filter, and the performance forecast filter. We can combine the three under a single concept of *managerial capability filter*, which we label M in Figure 10.2.

When the performance forecast finally reaches management, it will again be filtered by the management's *perception filter*, which we shall call K. If $M = K$, the management is likely to be very pleased with the forecast, even if it is totally unrealistic, because it confirms its beliefs and prejudices. If $K > M$, the management will regard the forecasts as too simplistic and restrictive and will seek a way to enrich them. If $K < M$ (the case illustrated in Figure 10.3), management will probably feel that the forecasters have engaged in 'blue sky', 'unrealistic' flights of fancy and seek to make the forecasts more 'practical', which means more consonant with past experiences and perceptions.

Nor will management necessarily welcome non-extrapolative performance forecasts. Depending on their culture, different managers will place different values on the past, the present, and the future. Such forecasting preferences by different managers will influence the choice of the 'official' expectations. We can describe this choice by the simple 'balance of power' formula:

$$E = \alpha D^{-t} + \beta_{P}{}^{0} + \gamma_{P}{}^{t}$$

$$\alpha + \beta + \gamma = 1$$

where E is the *managerial performance expectation* along some dimension of performance, P^{-t} is performance expectations by backward or past looking managers, P^{0} the performance expectation of managers who rely on the present, and P^{t} those of future-oriented managers.

We can interpret the formula in two ways; first, as reflecting the outcome of a group influence process. In this case, α, β, γ are the relative power coefficients of different managers. Or we can interpret it as the manner in which an individual manager balances the various respective inputs in arriving at his personal expectations. In this case, α, β, γ measure his individual propensities to rely on the past, the present, or the future.

In both cases, coefficients of α, β, γ are also descriptive of the culture. Thus:

$\beta = \gamma = 0$ in stable cultures in which an ESO will rely on the past;

$\gamma = 0$ in reactive cultures; the ESO lives in the past and the present;

$\alpha = 0$ in inquiring cultures; the ESO considers the past as an unreliable guide to the future;

$\alpha = \beta = 0$ in creative cultures; the ESO focuses on 'new futures'.

For mathematically inclined readers, we present in Figure 10.4 a formal model of the logical process.

The scanning process applies the scanning filter $\{A\}_M$ to obtain the perceived environment $\{A\}_F$:

$$\{A\}_F = \{A\}_T \cap \{A\}_M \cap \{A\}_M$$

The environmental forecast generates the demand function:

$$D_F = f_M(\{A\}_F)$$

where f_M denotes the forecasting technology of a managerial capability at level M.

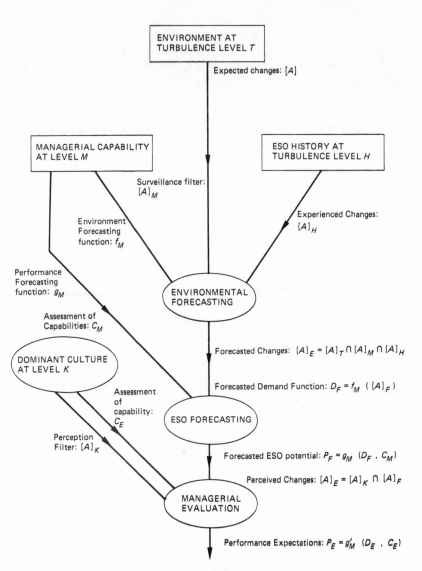

Figure 10.4   Process of Formation of Expectations

The performance forecast converts the demand into future performance:

$$P_F = g_M(D_F, C_M)$$

where g_M is the forecasting technology and C_M the assessment of the ESO s capabilities (' strengths and weaknesses').

Management next applies its cultural filter to the forecast by:

1. Changing the probable event set (which may impoverish or enrich the set $\{A\}_F$):

$$\{A\}_E = \{A\}_K \cap \{A\}_F$$

2. Adjusting the demand function: $D_E = f'_M(\{A\}_E)$;
3. Adjusting the estimate of the ESO strengths and weaknesses from C_M to C_E. (In the firm managers typically think the capability to be higher than do the analysts):
4. Adjusting the performance forecast to obtain $P_E = g'_M (D_E, C_E)$, which represents the managerial expectations.

In summary, we note that the model of expectations-formation developed above applies equally to ESOs in which expectations formation is a judgemental process, as well as to the ESO in which there are different types of managerial technology. We have already enunciated in words in Chapter 9 the basic hypothesis underlying the preceding development.

MODEL OF PERFORMANCE ASPIRATIONS

In Chapter 8 we have identified three influences which interact in formation of aspirations. These are the rational goals set forth by the management; the performance preferences of influential groups and individuals; and the forces of habit, tradition and past successes.

In the course of aspiration-forming behavior these three influences are frequently difficult to separate from one another. But for theory-building purposes we separate them in the manner shown in Figure 10.5. As in previous models, Figure 10.5 can be interpreted in two different ways. For ESOs such as the many firms which engage in explicit and formal objectives-setting, the figure can be viewed as a model of the objectives-setting process (which is usually followed later by implementation). For ESOs in which objectives are not made explicit, Figure 10.5 can be interpreted as a configuration of forces which is brought to bear, *after* the organizational results are in, on deciding whether the historical strategic behavior should be amended or continued.

For modelling purposes, we have separated the influential actors into two classes: the *managers*, whose role is to guide and control the various units entrusted to them, and *stakeholders* – other individuals and groups (both insiders and outsiders) – who have the power to influence the behavior of the ESO. Members of both classes seek to fulfill their personal performance aspirations through the results of the ESO. As we discussed previously (and as shown in Figure 10.5), the managers, unlike the stakeholders, have a conflict between their personal aspirations and the demands of their leadership role.

As we have already discussed, in typical non-profits managers abdicate the strategic leadership responsibility in favor of pursuing their personal goals and join the stakeholders in the political struggle. In terms of Figure 10.5 this means that managers do not exert a *performance drive*, even if they have the authority to do so. As a result, the oval labelled *managerial performance aspirations* is atrophied, and environmental expectations have no influence on the aspirations. This case corresponds to the model commonly found in sociological literature in which management is not recognised as a distinctive influential subclass.

At the opposite extreme are business firms in which managers are totally profit-motivated and the power is concentrated in the hands of top management. In this case the oval labelled *political aspirations* is atrophied, and the model describes purely profit-oriented behavior.

In a majority of firms and many non-profits the behavior lies between the two extremes. Both managerial leadership and political influence are important, but the managers, being human, divide their energies between acting as strategic leaders and playing the political game.

In all cases an additional influence on aspiration (shown at the bottom of Figure 10.5) is exerted by the strategic *culture*, the *capabilities*, and the history of the ESOs behavior. As we have discussed in detail in Chapter 8, the historical culture and the

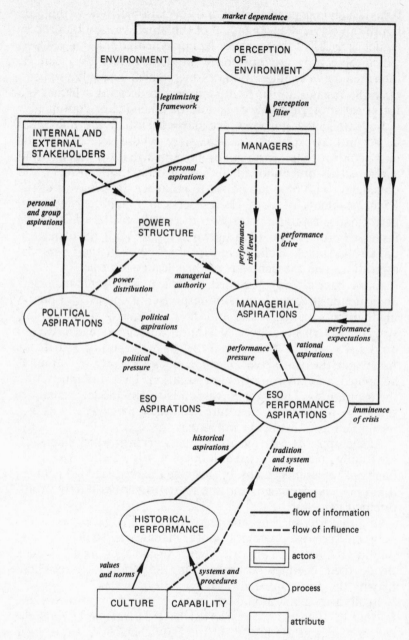

Figure 10.5   Formation of Performance Aspirations

capability of an ESO influence behavior through values and norms, institutionalized procedures, and formal management systems. These influences support and reinforce continuance of the past aspirations against the rational and the political preferences.

Figure 10.5 shows that a principal input to rational aspirations are the future *performance expectations* modelled in the preceding section. In converting these into aspirations conservative managers will reduce the aspiration levels to avoid risk; aggressive managers will do the opposite. As a result, the rational aspirations may end up below or above the expectations. This result will be influenced by four factors.

The first is the aggressiveness of the expectations institutionalized in the managerial roles. These are usually expressed through a combination of cultural norms and the relationship between rewards and performance. In the firm the culture norms typically call for maximal aggressiveness, in the not-for-profits for stable adequate income to perpetuate the ESO.

The second influence is the market dependence of the ESO. As we have discussed earlier, in the firm the market dependence is total. In a non-for-profit there is a total level of income which the ESO needs to continue survival, say A_r^T where r denotes 'managerial' and T 'total', and a fraction of it, say S, which comes from subsidy. Thus the not-for-profits need $(1-S)A_r^T$ from the market.

The third factor is the personal aggressiveness of the managers, which we have discussed under strategic leadership. In Figure 10.5 it is described by a combination of the *risk propensity* of the management, and the managerial *performance drive* which it is prepared to apply to the ESO.

The fourth factor is the *managerial authority* which management has within the power structure.

Combining these four factors, we can describe the managerial aspirations for the ESO:

$$A_r = A_r^T(1-S)+(E-A_r^T)\cdot p\cdot l\cdot a$$

where

A_r is the managerial aspiration;
A_r^T is the income needed for survival;

S is the fraction of A_r^T received from subsidies;
E is the performance expectation.

$0 \leq l \leq \alpha$ is a measure of aggressiveness of expectations institutionalized in the role;
$0 \leq l \leq \beta$ is a measure of the managerial performance drive;
$0 \leq a \leq 1$ is the strength of the managerial authority;
α and β, the upper limits of aggressiveness of the role and of managerial drive, will normally be less than 1, which means that the ESO scales its aspirations down to the expectations. But in aggressive maximizing firms α and β will be greater than one.

We can put the above expression in words:

HYPOTHESIS 10.1: DETERMINANTS OF MANAGERIAL PERFORMANCE

As a minimum, management seeks survival income;
In addition, it seeks a fraction of the difference between the performance expectations and survival which is proportional to:
    1. The expectations of the managerial role;
    2. The personal managerial drive;
    3. The managerial authority.

The last point (3) is included to account for the fact that most experienced aggressive and realistic managers will scale rational aspirations which they present to the rest of the ESO in proportion to the enforcement power they possess (Recall the hypothesis 'limits of managerial power' in Chapter 7.)

As Figure 10.5 shows, having formulated rational expectations, management injects them in an ESO-wide aspiration formation process. In support of the aspirations it applies *performance pressure* in which can be described, using the above definitions, as $r = a \cdot e$.

As Figure 10.5 shows, political aspirations are formed through a political influence process in which individuals and groups negotiate and/or bargain about their performance preferences. As discussed before, in decentralized power structures the bargaining is usually about levels of performance along accepted dimensions of aspirations. In distributed power structures the emphasis is more likely to be on reconciling preferences for different attributes which are important to the several power groups. Since rational aspirations (e.g. profitability) are frequently at odds with stakeholder aspirations (e.g. wages, employment security, power) in distributed power conditions, political aspirations will typically act to reduce the rational aspirations.

It is beyond the scope of this book to explore the detailed dynamics and varieties of the political influence process. For the purposes of the model we represent the outcome of negotiations and bargaining as a weighted average of the claims of the respective constituencies, in which the weighting factors are relative power potentials of each constituency. This can be expressed as follows:

$$A_P = \frac{1}{N} \sum_i^N p_i A_i$$

$$\sum_i^N p_i \leqq 1,$$

where A_p is the political aspiration level arrived at through the influence process, A_i are the aspirations of the respective power groups, and P_i are their influence potentials.

This influence interacts with the two others (the managerial pressure and the historical inertia/tradition) in the final choice of ESO aspirations, which we represent as follows:

$$A = (p A_P + h A_h) \cdot (1 - e^{-\alpha(E - C)} + r A_r)$$

where

$$(p + h) \cdot (1 - e^{-\alpha(E - C)}) + r = 1$$

HYPOTHESIS 10 In the above expressions:

$-p$ is a measure of the political pressure brought to bear by the stakeholders. It will be high in politically polarized, multi-ideological ESOs. In such ESOs the aspirations will be typically multidimensional, reflecting the variety of preferences. p will be very low in authoritarian power structures.

— h is a measure of the influence of past history. It will be high in highly structured, large, and old ESOs. It will be low in fluid, young, and small ESOs. It will be high relative to r in weakly managed ESOs.

— r is a measure of the managerial pressure toward managerial aspirations. It will be high when the political structure is authoritarian and the managers are strongly performance-motivated. It will also be high in decentralized power ESOs in which there is a strong common *esprit de corps*. The managerial pressure will be low in distributed power ESOs where management lacks the necessary authority. It will be low in ESOs in which management is unambitious and has an aversion to taking risks.

The mathematical complication in the above equation, added by the exponential term, is introduced to underline the impact of the basic survival hypothesis on the aspirations. It will be recalled that when survival is threatened, all ESOs close ranks and address the problem of perpetuating their existence. This causes the ESO to suppress the dysfunctional political aspirations, to disregard past tradition, and to focus behavior on the potential offered by the environment.

Such temporary suppression of politics and inertia is described by the expression $(1 - e^{-\alpha(E-C)})$. The term E is the expectations of the ESO, and C is the level of performance at which survival is threatened. When $E = C$ the above term becomes zero. As E becomes relatively larger, the expression in parenthesis tends toward 1, thus allowing for full impact of the non-rational influences.

The term $(0 \leq \alpha \leq 1)$ in the exponent is introduced to account for differences in organizational sensitivity to crisis. If α is small the ESO is highly sensitive and exaggerates the prospects of a crisis. If α is large the ESO is myopic to its prospects and will allow the expectations to approach the crisis level before it reacts. As discussed in the preceding chapter, the quality of the communications system has a strong influence in α.

We can express the above symbolic reasoning in words:

HYPOTHESIS 10.2: DETERMINANTS OF ORGANIZATIONAL ASPIRATIONS

The overall aspirations of an ESO are the result of a power process involving interaction of political influence and strategic leadership. The factors which contribute to the aspirations are:
—the managerial aspirations;
—aspirations of the influential stakeholders;
—the historical aspiration behavior.
When performance expectations approach a survival crisis level, rational aspirations become dominant.

CHOICE OF STRATEGIC THRUST

We recall (from Chapter 5) that different modes of strategic behavior can be described by the level of the strategic thrust. The choice of the thrust is influenced by the same factors as aspirations: the parochial preferences of the non-managerial stakeholders, the rational influence exerted by management, and the historical dynamics of the ESO. The cast of characters involved in the choice of thrust changes somewhat. The external stakeholders, who have a strong interest in the results, frequently have little concern for the internal process. Thus the power interaction is largely between the internal non-managerial stakeholders and the managers.

We have shown earlier (in Chapter 5) that economic results and strategic behavior are interrelated. A horizontal line drawn on the lower part of Fig. 5.13 would show that a given level of performance can be attained by only a limited range of strategic modes. When behavior is outside this range, performance drops off. When management exercises its strategic leadership role, it attempts to match performance aspirations and strategic behavior, so that attainment of performance goals is both probable and possible.

Definition: The thrust selected by the strategic leadership as the best suited to meet the managerial performance aspirations shall be called the *preferred managerial thrust*.

Definition: The thrust selected as a result of the political influence process within the ESO shall be called the *preferred political thrust*.

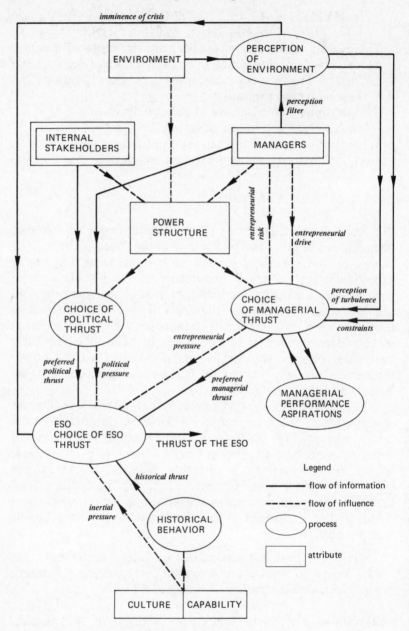

Figure 10.6   Choice of Strategic Thrust

The choice of the managerial thrust is illustrated in the right-hand part of Figure 10.6. It is influenced by the following factors:

1. The level of rational performance aspirations A_r which the management is trying to achieve.
2. The perception by management of the level of the environmental turbulence. This, as we have discussed previously, may be misjudged. In myopic, and even in tuned-in ESOs under changing environmental turbulence, management is likely to misperceive the future climate.
3. The perception by management of the thrust which will best permit attainment of aspirations. In our earlier discussion of culture, we have noted that work-determined cultures tend to perceive their preferred thrust as being the key to organizational success, independently of the needs of the environment. This leads to differences in preferences between general management and managers of various specialized units. Each, trying to assure the success of his area of responsibility, is likely to make a different choice. The general management will opt for matching the thrust to the turbulence, unit managers will opt for thrusts which will optimize the results of their respective functions. In concrete terms, this means that units will have preferences for strategic thrusts which correspond to their work culture.
4. Since a given level of aspirations can usually be attained by a range of strategic behaviors, the choice of the preferred thrust will further be influenced by the management assessment of the fit between different thrusts and the capabilities of the ESO. (In business planning literature this is called 'maximizing strengths and minimizing weaknesses'.) If the ESO has been successful in the past and the environmental turbulence had remained steady, this assessment is likely to be quite accurate. But a recent lack of success or changing turbulence usually make it difficult to identify the best match between the strategic thrust and the ESOs capability. (A technology for identification of such match, called *strategic planning* has been in existence for some twenty years. But to date its applications have been limited to a small percentage of the business firms and a few non-profits.)
5. The energy and the drive which management brings to

matching aspirations and strategic behavior will be important. In Figure 10.6, we have described this as a combination of *entrepreneurial risk propensity* and *entrepreneurial drive* to distinguish them from the comparable but different attributes of performance drive and performance risk propensity of Figure 10.5. It will be recalled from our discussion of strategic leadership that it is not infrequent to encounter performance-oriented managers who have no entrepreneurial propensities. Such managers focus their energies on trying to 'squeeze' performance from an ESO, while accepting a strategic behavior which no longer holds the necessary performance potential.

6. As in setting performance aspirations, the management's ability to make its influence felt depends on the extent of its *managerial authority*. It will recalled from previous discussion that greater managerial power is needed to change strategic behavior than the change the level of aspirations. Further, it will be recalled that changes in budgets are easier to introduce than change in thrust. Therefore managers with limited authority confine their attitudes to aspirations and budgeting, but leave the strategic thrust alone.

7. Finally, we recall from discussion of the rules of the game that, increasingly, external *constraints* affect the choice of the thrust. The not-for-profits have been traditionally narrowly limited in their strategic degrees of freedom; and the business firms are increasingly being limited by governmental and social pressures.

As we turn attention to the left-hand side of Figure 10.6, choice of the preferred political thrust is similar to the formation of political performance aspirations and we shall not repeat the description here. A significant point is that, unlike the managerial thrust where an attempt is made to relate the thrust to the performance aspirations, the political thrust is typically chosen *independently* of the political performance aspirations. On the contrary, a preference for 'more money (high aspirations) and less work (low thrust)' is a widely prevalent human condition.

HYPOTHESIS 10.3: INCONSISTENCY OF POLITICAL THRUST AND PERFORMANCE ASPIRATIONS

In distributed power organizations, political performance

aspirations and the preferred political thrust aspirations will be typically contradictory.

The third influence on the choice of thrust, as Figure 10.6 shows, is brought to bear by the historical culture, capability, and tradition. Again, as in performance aspirations, these attributes exert a passive inertial force which reinforces the historical behavior. The strength of this force is proportional to the historical success of the ESO in meeting its aspirations.

We model the interaction of the three major influences in a way very similar to the performance aspirations:

$$T = (\pi T_\pi + \eta T_\eta)(1 + e^{-\beta(E-C)}) + \rho T_r$$

where

T is the thrust chosen by the ESO;
π is the political pressure;
η is the inertial pressure;
T_π and T_η respectively, are the preferred political thrust and the historical thrust;
ρ is the entreprenurial pressure;
T_r is the preferred managerial thrust.

Just as in the case of performance aspirations, the bracketed expression containing the exponential is introduced to recognize the fact that, as prospects of non-survival increase, the inertial and political influence tend to give way to the rational choice. In the exponential we have used the coefficient $\beta < \alpha$ (See Figure 10.5) to indicate that ESOs are more *performance-sensitive* than they are *behavior-sensitive*; that is, they turn to a rational choice of aspirations sooner than they abandon their politically/ historically determined behavior. We shall have more to say about this in Chapters 11 and 12.

Although the two formulas for the thrust are very similar in form, the chosen thrust T will not necessarily be adequate to reach the chosen aspirations A, particularly during changes in environmental turbulence. Therefore, behaviors in support of a process of reconciliation of A and of T may come in conflict. If $\rho \approx 1$, and the ESO has a strategic planning system, management has both the system and the authority to reconcile A and T

during the planning cycle. In more typical cases (when strategic planning is lacking and politics and tradition are strong), the reconciliation occurs through experience, trial, and error, which is schematically illustrated in Figure 10.7. In the following chapter we turn to exploring this reconciliation process in some detail.

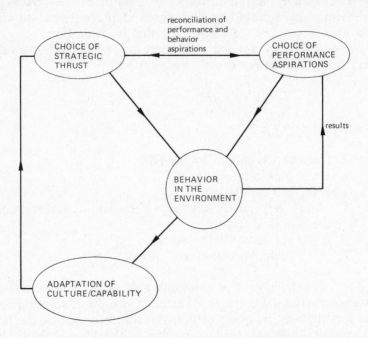

Figure 10.7   Process of Reconciliation of Performance and Behavior Aspirations

HYPOTHESIS 10.4: MISMATCH OF ASPIRATIONS AND THRUST

In ESOs in which the managerial authority is weak, performance aspirations and the thrust are likely to be mismatched in the sense that the thrust will not be the best suited for attaining the performance aspirations.

11 Transition Behavior

'There is nothing more difficult to take in hand, more perilous to conduct, than to take a lead in the introduction of a new order of things, because the innovation has for enemies all those who have done well under the old conditions and lukewarm defenders in those who may do well under the new.'

Machiavelli

LAG RESPONSE TO ENVIRONMENTAL CHANGE

In this chapter we turn attention to the process by which ESOs change strategic behavior. In a majority of cases the change is triggered by events in the outside environment, but strategic change is also frequently caused by internal power shifts. We start our discussion with the environmentally induced change.

In all ESOs, even strategically stable ones, change is an ongoing process. On every orbit of our turbulence model developed in Chapter 5, ESOs cope daily with disturbance induced by the environment and disharmonies in the internal configuration. In fact, were it not for change, there would be no logical justification for the existence of managers/administrators.

In this book, we have focused attention on a particular type of change called 'strategic', which affects either the internal configuration or the external thrust of the ESO. In this chapter we further focus on changes which are major departures from those previously experienced in the environment. We have analysed the profile of such changes in Chapter 5. The profile may consist of the evolution of a singular discontinuous *breakthrough* event, as in our transistor example; or it may consist of a coherent, cumulative series of events, which is usually called a *trend*. An example is the current evolution of the legislation which is progressively redefining the freedoms and the power of management within the firm.

As we discussed in Chapter 9, the response of an ESO to an environmental change is myopic in change-resisting cultures and foresightful in change-seeking ones. We start with the myopic organizations. In such organizations there is no mechanism for advance identification of environmental changes. The change is recognized through performance results. Thus there is an *identification delay* between the time at which performance drops below the aspiration level and the time management is informed about it. This is a systemic delay due in part to the time consumed in recording, interpreting, collating, and transmitting information, and in another part to the time consumed by the responsible managers in communicating with one another and agreeing on the response.

Once management becomes aware that performance has dropped below the aspiration level, it may allow further delays. One of these is a *verification delay*. Since performance is typically not a smooth but rather an oscillating curve, management may feel that the unwelcome performance departure is due to a statistical variation and not a fundamental case, and that it will 'work itself out' with time.

If powerful managers feel that recognition of the performance deficiencies will endanger their position or reflect negatively on their reputation, they will cause a *political delay*. Even if they are convinced that the threat is real, such managers will fight a delaying action, seeking scapegoats, developing a line of defense or retreat.

Finally, if the negative results are caused by a novel and unfamiliar event, a *cultural delay* will occur. Managements whose culture is inconsistent with the signals coming from the environment will treat the event as irrelevant and again express confidence that the trouble will 'work itself out'.

In a given situation, all four causes may contribute to a delay in response which we shall jointly call a *procrastination* delay. They may be concurrent or additive. The verbal justification for them will usually be based on the need for verification and identification, even if the cultural and political concerns happen to be the real 'hidden agenda'.

Thus the news that performance has dropped below aspirations is followed by a period of negotiations, discussions, and re-evaluations. During this period the ESO will continue its strategically stable or reactive behavior and the performance will continue to drop. Finally, a consensus is reached that a departure from the historical behavior is necessary.

We label the point of consensus by A_2 in Figure 11.1, where the lower curve shows the cumulating operating losses which occur during the procrastination period $A_1 - A_2$. The upper part of the figure shows the curve of marginal costs incurred in coping with the change. As the figure shows, no extra cost is incurred during the procrastination period.

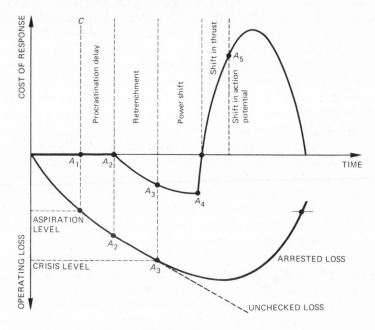

Figure 11.1   Lag Response to Threat

In a stable ESO a typical reaction is to turn to internal retrenchment: cost reduction, freeze on hiring, cessation of management development programs, cutback in research and development. The first to be cut are activities which do not have a short-term payoff, or are not direct contributors to the productive operations of the ESO. Paradoxically, these cuts are usually applied first to investment in the entrepreneurial potential (R & D budget) – the key investment which is needed to respond to the change.

A reactive ESO may accompany internal retrenchment by

attempts to revive the sagging external demand for its output. The measures taken are defensive, designed to make the ESOs products less expensive and more attractive to customers: a new advertising campaign, price cuts, price rebates, new financing terms. The essential nature of both the internal market and the responses is that they are focused on adjustment of budgets without any substantial changes in the character of the programs.

The internal and external retrenchments will succeed if the drop in performance is the result of 'competitive flabbiness' on the part of the ESO: a loss of efficiency in its internal operations or of marketing aggressiveness. But if the cause is a change in the structure of the environment which calls for changes in products, technology, or markets, retrenchment will not arrest the performance decline, as shown by the segment $A_2 - A_3$ on the lower graph of Figure 11.1. The companion segment on the upper graph shows that the costs of responses do not increase, and will typically drop somewhat.

As retrenchment proceeds, management gradually becomes convinced that 'competition flabbiness' is not the cause of the trouble and that retrenchment will not arrest the continuing decline. The process of arriving at this conviction is similar to the initial procrastination period. There are no unambiguous signs of the failure of the retrenchment strategy, but rather an accumulation of reverses, punctuated by minor successes. The delay in recognizing the failure of retrenchment is determined by the same factors as during the procrastination delay, plus the gravity of the new departure which the ESO must now make. For a stable ESO any departure from budgeting is a major one, and even minor product changes represent an escalation of the historical strategic thrust. Such escalation violates the prevalent cultural norms and is fraught with perceived risk and imponderables. Any substantial change looms as a major discontinuity from the past. Such perception was prevalent for example, in the Ford Motor Company in the late 1920s when, after more than twenty-five years of leadership with the Model T, it had to confront the fact that the age of the Model T had come to an end.

Because of the compounded reluctance to act an ESO frequently persists in retrenchment until the situation deteriorates into a crisis. Perception of a crisis (at point A_3) triggers a new, more drastic response. The crisis atmosphere causes psychological anxiety, social and political upheavals. As discussed before, shared anxiety about survival and security acts to unify the ESO. Forces of habit and tradition are suspended, and personal and political preferences are suppressed during a common search for survival.

But, having exhausted the repertoire of familiar and tested responses, the organization is now at a loss for a solution. The leadership which put the ESO through a succession of failures is discredited. As a result, a search starts for a 'savior' individual or group which promises to lead the ESO out of its predicament. This diverts organizational energy from the search for a strategic solution to a realignment and transfer of power. If no promising group or individual is found inside, the ESO turns to the outside for new talent. Typically, the external stakeholders, who in normal times exercise only a nominal influence on the ESO, assume a controlling role. In business firms, for example, the board comes to life, fires the discredited management, and puts new talent in its place.

Once the new leadership is installed, attention turns back to the mounting losses (at point A_4). The measures taken by the new leaders are likely to be contradictory. On the one hand, there will be a continuation of retrenchment – a further search for reduction in the cost of doing business. On the other hand, there will now be a determined effort to realign the strategic thrust with the environment – an activity which requires budgets which are way and above the retrenchment levels. As a result, 'least-costs solutions' will be sought. This leads the ESO to concentrate on the needs of the market place and to neglect the necessary costly companion changes in the internal strategic action potential. The perception of the new management is that 'fat is being cut off the muscle', while the strategic thrust is being revitalized. In actuality, the 'muscle is being cut to the bone'.

As shown by the upper curve of Figure 11.1, past point A_4 the aggregate expenditures on strategic activity rise dramatically. The ESO may now be engaged in a complete substitution of product technology, a discontinuous change in the marketing strategy, major withdrawals from unprofitable markets, divestment from obsolete parts of the organization, diversification into new areas of activity.

Frequently, these measures not only fail to arrest the losses but only serve to increase them. When this occurred in the Du Pont company after its diversification into the paint business, one disappointed officer wrote to another: 'It is a strange thing that the more paint we sell, the more money we lose.'

We have diagnosed earlier that the success of a new thrust is limited by the supporting strategic action potential. If the latter is out of line with the thrust, even the optimal thrust will fail to produce results. But this is typically not clear in an ESO launched on a change of thrust under crisis. The ESO continues trying 'to sell more paint', ascribing its difficulties to imperfections of the new strategy. Eventually the 'strategy-structure gap' becomes recognized and the ESO turns its attention to bringing the capabilities and the strategic culture in line with the thrust. We have indicated this transition at point A_5 on Figure 11.1. As the internal configuration becomes aligned with the external thrust, things begin to improve and the performance returns to the aspiration level. When this occurs, strategic activity is reduced and the ESO stabilizes its behavior at the new thrust level.

Such return to the earlier aspiration levels is a favorable scenario for the outcome of a strategic shift. In the course of this century a majority of business firms have successfully followed this scenario twice: first in the early 1900s when behavior shifted from entrepreneurial to the stable/reactive; and again in the 1930s when some firms shifted to the anticipatory behavior and others to the exploring.

But the favorable outcome is not universal. Under another scenario the change of the strategic thrust produces enough performance improvement to dissipate a feeling of crisis. If the ESO is weakly managed from the top, traditional political and cultural forces reassert themselves before the strategic culture has moved to a new level. These forces cause a regression back to the earlier strategic thrust and the ESO becomes a candidate for another crisis.

Under a third scenario, the ESO is unable to solve its problem. This may occur through an adverse configuration of the following factors:

1. If the ESO starts the thrust change too late to catch up with the threat (say, recapture a lost market);
2. If it starts too late to close the gap between the strategic thrust and capability/culture;
3. If the ESO lacks the human and financial resources necessary to close the gap;

4. If the change in turbulence has changed the industry into a strategic trap.

If one or more of the above conditions occurs, and if the environmental disturbance affects a majority of the ESOs income, the ESO will go bankrupt. If only a part of the income is affected, the ESO will survive but will be forced to reduce drastically its level of aspirations.

The sequence of events in stable ESOs illustrated in Figure 11.1 applies, with modifications, to the reactive ESO. Like the stable ESO, the reactive organizations respond to change after its impact begins to be felt. But the procrastination delay after the aspiration level has been broached is likely to be shorter. Furthermore, a reactive ESO is not averse to change like a stable one, it is prepared to 'roll with the punches'. The initial repertoire of responses includes not only budgetary retrenchment measures but positive strategic moves to improve the situation. Thus after the General Motors Company felt the impact of the compact car, it increased strategic budgets, introduced product improvements, intensified advertising campaigns. But just as in a stable ESO, the repertoire of the initial measures is limited by the historical strategic culture and the historical perception of the environment. The ESO seeks to rectify the situation within the limits of its prior experience and understanding of the environment. Generally, when familiar responses fail to rectify the situation, a reactive ESO will begin a search for alternatives long before crisis becomes imminent. Power shifts are much less frequent, and a strategic shift is triggered in an atmosphere of positive commitment, rather than crisis.

Thus a reactive ESO will respond sooner, will go through a retrenchment more quickly and, if it is insufficient, will launch a strategic shift earlier than a stable ESO. By virtue of an earlier and more sensitive response, reactive ESOs are less likely to wait for a crisis and are able to make a deliberate planned shift, as did General Motors in launching its multi-billion product revamping campaign.

The lag response behavior described above has been widely discussed in sociological literature. The model presented by Cyert and March is one well-known example. Readers familiar with Cyert and March will recognize the essential differences between our and their treatment. They deal with behavior which occurs prior to point A_2 in Figure 11.1, and therefore confine their attention to what we have called the budgeting behavior. Our effort has been to extend the description to strategic behavior. Our model has many features in common with the recent work of Schendell, and Hedberg and Starbuck.

We summarize the behavior of change-resisting ESOs by means of the following hypotheses:

HYPOTHESIS 11.1: INITIAL RESPONSE OF CHANGE-RESISTING ESOs

1. Change-resisting ESOs react after the impact of turbulence has reduced performance below aspiration levels.
2. The first reaction is a procrastination delay followed by measures consistent with prior experience and ESO culture. In stable ESOs these are changes in budgets, in reactive ESOs incremental strategic measures.

HYPOTHESIS 11.2: POWER SHIFT

When the initial response leads to a crisis, the secondary response is a shift in power.

HYPOTHESIS 11.3: SEQUENCE OF STRATEGIC SHIFT

The tertiary response is a strategic shift, which follows a typical Chandlerian strategy-structure sequence.

LEAD RESPONSE TO CHANGE

The response to change in change-seeking cultures (anticipating-exploring-creative) is closer to the microeconomic than to the sociological model. It is largely found among aggressive firms which are goal-seeking and are open to the environment.

A characteristic shared by the change-seeking cultures is that they typically respond before and not after the event. We have already discussed on several occasions that the anticipating culture is limited in its perspective to extrapolation of the past, whereas exploring and creative cultures look for the unfamiliar. But all three engage in forecasting (formally or informally), which gives them advanced warning of impending changes. Such a forecast is illustrated in the upper part of Figure 11.2, in which an ESO discovers that at time *t* in the future a consequential change will begin to impact on the ESO.

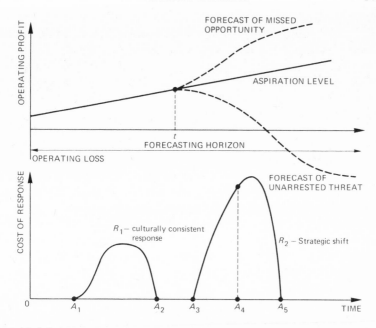

Figure 11.2   Lead Response to Environmental Change

In an effort to take advantage (or forestall a negative impact) of the change, change-seeking ESOs initiate a response in advance of the event. But premature commitment has the drawback that it is triggered on imperfect information which will improve with time. Future development of the change will shed new light on the importance of the change and also provide better information for selection of the response. Therefore managers of change-seeking ESOs apply a 'delay principle' made famous by General Eisenhower: they do not trigger the response until the point at which further delay would begin to reduce the timeliness and the effectiveness of the response.

The choice of the initial measures is compatible with the respective cultures. An anticipating ESO (such as, say, the General Electric Company) has a history of aggressive strategic change and will not limit itself to retrenchment or budget changes. Instead, it will select the response which appears appropriate to the nature and impact of the change. Furthermore, such ESOs typically have well-developed analytic capabilities and would not rely on the trial and error, one-at-a-time approach of the change-resisting ESO. A number of alternatives would be examined and the most promising ones selected for implementation.

But the repertoire of the measures considered by an anticipating ESO will be limited to logical extrapolations of the historical and familiar model of the environment. In this respect anticipating and reactive behaviors are alike.

If the results of the response show that the measures taken do not produce a satisfactory result, the anticipating ESO confronts the need for a strategic shift. At this point the historically-based rationality becomes an obstacle rather than a help in the next step. A paraphrase of the quotation from Whitehead presented at the head of our first chapter becomes applicable:

> The man with a method good for the purposes of his dominant (historical) interests is a pathological case in respect to his wider judgement on the coordination of this method with a more complex experience.

Thus, on the threshold of a strategic shift, an anticipating ESO may exhibit an even greater tendency to procrastinate than a reactive ESO which is less committed to a structured 'method' of viewing the environment.

We have illustrated the cost consequences of response in the lower part of Figure 11.2. The period $0 - A_1$ is the prudent 'Eisenhower delay'. The first cost curve from A_1 to A_2 represents the intracultural response, which in this case is assumed to lead to unsatisfactory results. $A_2 - A_3$ is the procrastination delay (which in change-seeking cultures occurs after the intracultural response, whereas change-resisting cultures procrastinate before responding at all). $A_3 - A_4$ is the cost of the change in strategic thrust, and $A_4 - A_5$ is the period during which attention shifts to the strategic action potential.

Anticipating ESOs have historically tended to be Chandlerian in their 'strategy-structure' sequence. An interesting development observable today in a number of intelligent anticipatory firms (e.g. General Electric, Sears) is the emergence of a tendency to reverse the sequence. These ESOs are beginning to concern themselves with the strategic action potential as a subject in itself and not as a consequence of disappointments with a new strategic thrust.

The response of the exploring and creative ESO differs from the anticipatory in the fact that, thanks to their broader cultures, they accept a wider repertoire of discontinuity from a past experience. As a result, when the environment is highly turbulent they are less likely to select an initial ineffective response R_1 of Figure 11.2. Instead, they will start with R_2, which will save them both time and money. On the other hand, if a major *de-escalation* of turbulence is taking place (for example, an industry settling into a steady growth period after a turbulent entrepreneurial birth), the inquiring/creative ESOs are likely to over-respond by over-emphasizing strategic change when a shift to operating efficiency and strategic stability is indicated. Their first response R_1 will typically be innovate and hence ineffective in the new environ-ment, and the subsequent response R_2 will be a stabilizing shift to a lower level of thrust.

Because American cultural norms assign a positive value to enterpreneurship, we need to recall once again that lead behavior is not necessarily superior to lag behavior. The success of either depends on the environment in which the ESO operates. In stable or reactive environments, which are not subject to violent environmental transitions, the change-resisting behaviors offer the advantage of economic efficiency, and lag behavior will produce superior results.

Nor are reactive ESOs necessarily non-aggressively managed. As we have shown in Chapter 9, managerial leadership is a combination of a *performance drive* and an *entrepreneurial drive*. In a successful stable/reactive business firm one typically finds a strong performance drive, while the entrepreneurial drive is weak. This behavior has produced many outstanding successes (e.g. Henry Ford I from 1900–29). History is also full of examples of failure by these same successes to introduce a timely strategic shift when the environmental turbulence shifted to a higher level (e.g. the failure of Henry Ford I in 1930 to recognize the basic shift in the nature of the automative business).

HYPOTHESIS 11.4: RESPONSE OF CHANGE-SEEKING ESOs

Change-seeking ESOs respond to a shift in turbulence before the fact. The first response is consistent with the ESOs culture, the second triggers a strategic shift.

STRATEGIC SURPRISE

During the past thirty years growth of management technology has substantially raised the level of forecasting and planning skills available to ESO. As a result, the time perspective of business firms, where much of this new technology was born, continued to extend further and further into the future. From one-year budgets a majority of middle and large-sized firms moved to long-range planning with horizons of three, five, or ten years. It was generally assumed that a firm could plan as far ahead as it felt necessary.

The petroleum crisis dealt a severe blow to this optimistic assumption. A number of firms which planned well into the future were, nevertheless, strategically surprised. Studies conducted after the crisis showed that in part the surprise was due to the firm's failure to use appropriate forecasting technology, but primarily it was due to the narrow cultural perception filter of managers. But, as we have discussed in the preceding chapters, these studies also showed that the petroleum crisis was a symptom of a general escalation of turbulence. A primary characteristic of this escalation is that momentous events surface and develop at a rapid rate. For change-resisting ESOs, which respond after the fact, this means that the time remaining for response is progressively shrinking. For change-seeking ESOs, which seek to respond before the fact, this means that the limits of forecasting the time horizons are shrinking, that these limits cannot be overcome through improvements of forecasting technology, and that the time available for advanced response to events is becoming progressively shorter.

As a result, ESOs will increasingly have to cope with rapidly developing and unfamiliar events which we shall call strategic surprises.

Definition: A *Strategic Surprise* is an event which:
1. Arrives unannounced, which means that it is filtered out by the ESOs environmental scanning activity until after the impact is felt by the ESO;
2. Is not only sudden but novel (which is one of the reasons why the filters exclude it);
3. Implies a major impact on the performance of the ESO;
4. Develops rapidly, leaving little time for trial, error and experimentation.

In terms of Figure 11.1, when all four of these factors are present, the unchecked loss curve drops so rapidly that the crisis point A_3 is reached very quickly after the aspiration levels A_1. For change-resisting cultures this means a certain survival crisis.

In terms of Figure 11.2, a strategic surprise means that the forecasting horizon t is substantially shorter than the time span $A_1 - A_2$. Thus in change-seeking ESOs a surprise, as a minimum, forces a crash response and, as a maximum, a survival crisis.

As we have shown in Chapter 5, many of the potential strategic surprises can be avoided if ESOs turn from their historical reliance on strong signals and increase reliance on early *weak signals* of the incipient changes. To make use of weak signals it is essential to develop new environmental surveillance and planning technologies. It is also necessary to broaden the repertoire of ESO responses to include *weak signals* which progressively increase in strength as environmental signs become stronger.

This new technology is in the early stages of development. One such development is described in the author's paper on weak signals cited in the references at the end of this book. The awareness of the need for such technology is just emerging in business firms. A recent survey of a large sample of U.S. company presidents conducted by the American Management Association shows that the respondents are worried by the growing turbulence and unpredictability of the future. They forecast that a management will manage more conservatively in the future. They also see a reduction in innovation and a diversification of strategic risks. One respondent said that in the future management will 'increasingly manage by the balance sheet instead of by the operating statement.'

These views by leading managers reinforce our earlier hypothesis (6.4) that change-seeking and environmentally responsive ESOs will increasingly reverse the Chandlerian sequence. Increasingly 'structure' will become more flexible and responsive. Increasingly 'strategy' will be deferred until rapidly moving threats and opportunities become sufficiently visible to permit a calculated response.

HYPOTHESIS 11.5: STRATEGIC SURPRISE
An ESO is forced into a crisis response when the time that is

remaining for response is shorter than the time needed to execute the response through the existing systems and procedures.

SOCIAL INERTIA

In earlier discussion we recognized that expectations are typically not shared by all participants of an ESO. General management and middle managers (e.g. in marketing and R & D), whose roles involve direct concern with the environment, are likely to be very much better informed about the impending changes in the environment than are the internally oriented managers and the internally focused technostructure. The discrepancy in the respective perceptions is a function of the quality of the internal communication system.

If communications are poor, general management will become convinced of the seriousness and urgency of the situation before the rest of the ESO. If, as is usually the case, general management triggers a strategic shift before the rest of the ESO has become convinced of the imminence of a crisis, it usually encounters strong organizational resistance. The causes of this resistence are by now familiar from prior discussion: the inertia of the established systems, the cultural behavior preferences of powerful groups and individuals, the fear of loss of reputation and of power.

Cultures which are most threatened and which also stand to lose power will be the most resistant to change. But units to which the change is culturally acceptable may still resist the change for political reasons. For example, in a business firm, a change from stable to reactive behavior may be vigorously resisted by the production department if the change implies loss of power to the accounting and control department. But a more drastic change to the anticipatory behavior, through introduction of long-range planning, may be more acceptable, if it permits the production department to retain its power.

In Figure 11.3 we have constructed several combinations of cultural and political threats. As the figure shows, the greatest resistance to change will occur when an environmental change implies simultaneously a change in culture and a redistribution of power. At the other extreme, the change will be welcomed by the influential groups if it is culturally acceptable and reinforces the power of these groups.

In Figure 11.3 we labelled the resistance *social inertia*, because of its similarity to the inertia of physical bodies. The similarity is closest to the component of resistance contributed by the ESOs technology, systems, structures, and procedures. We shall call this the *systemic* component of social inertia. Just as in physical bodies, it depends on the physical, systemic, and structural properties of an ESO. The systemic component is a property of the organizational capabilities and is not directly affected by the dynamics of change.

POLITICAL IMPACT / CULTURAL IMPACT	POLITICALLY THREATENING	POLITICALLY NEUTRAL	POLITICALLY WELCOME
CHANGE IN CULTURE	GREATEST RESISTANCE	DEPENDS ON SIZE OF CULTURAL CHANGE	DEPENDS ON SIZE OF CULTURAL CHANGE
CULTURALLY ACCEPTABLE	DEPENDS OF SIZE OF THREAT	LEAST RESISTANCE	POSITIVE REINFORCEMENT

Figure 11.3   Relation of Social Inertia to Power and Culture

But as we have already discussed above, social inertia is also manifested through cultural and political resistance, and these components, as discussed in Chapter 10, vary as a function of the anxiety about survival. When a crisis appears imminent, political and cultural ambitions are suppressed. When the state of crisis is lifted, the political-cultural resistance returns.

Like physical inertia, the social inertial force is determined by the speed of the strategic shift. The greater the change in the strategic thrust impressed on the ESO during a given time interval, the greater will be the inertia. When the shift is slow and confined to isolated parts of an ESO, it passes unnoticed in other parts. The sense of 'it cannot happen to us' prevails. But when a rapid shift pervades the ESO, social and political differences are forgotten, and previously conflicting groups unite in a fight against an unwelcome change.

> *Definition*: *Social Inertia* is the resistance to change which arises in an ESO when an effort is made to change its strategic thrust. The components of inertia are systemic, cultural, and political.

A concise mathematical description of physical inertia was given by Isaac Newton in his famous laws of motion. In the first law he postulated that physical bodies tend to remain in rectilinear steady motion unless disturbed by a force. In the second law he postulated that the resistance to a change in motion is proportional to the rate of acceleration; and in the third that every action produces an equal and appropriate reaction.

With modifications we can adapt Newton's laws to the phenomenon of social inertia. As previously discussed, ESOs have a tendency to persist in the strategic thrust which is compatible with the dominant culture. In terms of of our orbital model in Chapter 5, this means that once an ESO has adapted its thrust to a level of turbulence, it tends to preserve that thrust.

To adapt Newton's second law, we introduce the concept of variable inertia (which, in fact, is done for physical bodies in Einstein's reformulation of Newton's laws). This can be described by the following equation. For each organizational unit within the ESO we can write:

$$i = I \cdot \left[1 - ae^{-\beta(E-C)} \right] \cdot \frac{B_A - B}{\Delta t}$$

where

i is the inertial force;

B is the preferred strategic thrust of the unit, determined by its culture;

B_A is the strategic thrust toward which it is being forced;

Δt is the time period in which the shift is being attempted;

β as before, is a crisis sensitivity coefficient;

$(E-C)$ as before, is a measure of the imminence of crisis.

An examination of the equation shows that at crisis, when $(E-C)$ the socio-political inertia is at a minimum, the expression becomes

$$\text{Inertial force} = I \cdot (1-a) \cdot \frac{B_A - B}{\Delta t}$$

Thus the term $I \cdot (1-a)$ is a measure of the systemic inertia, whereas the term I is the maximal inertia of the unit when the crisis is not imminent, and $\dfrac{1}{1-a}$ is a relative measure of the maximum socio-political inertia.

Newton's third law can be restated to say that the social inertia does not become evident until strategic leadership attempts to change the ESOs strategic thrust. In Chapter 10 we have already described this thrust-changing force as the *entrepreneurial pressure*, given by the following equation:

$$r = a \cdot \rho,$$

where

r is the entrepreneurial pressure;

a as before, is the strength of managerial authority;

ρ is the strength of the management's entrepreneurial drive.

The entrepreneurial action r produces an equal inertial reaction i. The action and reaction will occur in each unit of an ESO, but the strength of the respective forces will differ.

If there are j culturally distinctive units in the ESO which are involved in a change of thrust, we can write for each unit:

$$r_j = i_j$$

and, substituting previous expressions:

$$a_j \rho_j = I_j \left[I - a_j e^{-\beta_j(E-C)} \right] \cdot \frac{B_A - B_j}{\Delta t_j}$$

We recall that the entrepreneurial pressures are actions of respective unit managers, who attempt to guide ESOs toward a strategic thrust B_A in the face of unit preferences for behaviors B_j. In a weakly managed ESO the entrepreneurial activities of unit managers are likely to be poorly coordinated. At an extreme, in a distributed power ESO, there may not even be an agreement on the ultimate strategic thrust B_A; or an agreement may lack on a common time target Δt. In such cases the balances of forces in each unit will not be reconciled with the balance in others, each manager will set his own pace, and the change in thrust will be unbalanced, some units lagging behind the others. The transformation times Δt_j will be determined by the local power balances.

In a strongly managed ESO, general management will attempt to assess the force balances in each unit and develop a coordinated program through which the overall change in thrust (or in action potential) is accomplished on a common time schedule. This will involve applying extra entrepreneurial pressure on units with higher inertia, that is, units for which $B_A - B_j$ is the greatest. But, as discussed before, the entrepreneurial pressure is limited by the strength of managerial authority described by coefficients a_j. Hence there is a minimum transformation time, which we call Δt, which is required in a given power structure. We can derive approximate expression for this minimum feasible time in the following manner.

First, we sum all of the entrepreneurial and the inertial forces:

$$\sum_{j=I}^{N} a_i \cdot \rho_j = \sum_{j=1}^{N} I_j \cdot \left[1 - a_j e^{-\beta_j(E-C)} \right] \cdot \frac{B_A - B_j}{\Delta t}$$

and then solve for Δt:

$$\Delta t = \frac{\sum_{j}^{N} I_j \cdot \left[1 - a_{je} e^{-\beta_j(E-C)} \right] \cdot (B_A - B_j)}{\sum_{}^{N} a_j \rho_j}$$

(One of the key features of a management system called *strategic planning*, which we have discussed earlier, is to assure a timely and coordinated change in strategic thrust.)

For non-mathematical readers we can summarize the preceding discussion as follows:

HYPOTHESIS 11.6: SOCIAL INERTIA

1. An attempt to change an established strategic thrust induces organizational resistance in the form of delays, inefficiencies, and efforts to roll back the change.
2. The resistance is proportional to the complexity and rigidity of the ESOs structure and systems and to the political threat it presents to the key power centers, and is inversely proportional to the cultural acceptability of the new thrust.

HYPOTHESIS 11.7: ELASTICITY OF INERTIA

In a given ESO the resistance to change will vary with the imminence of a crisis. It will be least under actual crisis conditions.

HYPOTHESIS 11.8: SPEED OF TRANSFORMATION

The time required to effect a transformation of thrust varies directly with the inertial resistance and the size of the shift in the thrust. It varies inversely with the entrepreneurial pressure.

STRATEGIC DRIFT

In the earlier sections of this chapter, we have discussed rapid and highly visible strategic shift which occurs under pressure of a rapid environmental change. We next turn our attention to a less dramatic, slow, strategic shift which is less visible and frequently difficult to perceive. It acts like a process of gradual erosion, in the course of which both the external thrust and the strategic action potential are shifted to another level.

One condition under which such erosion occurs is in the wake of a premature relaxation of crisis atmosphere during a rapid shift in the strategic thrust. During a crisis shift, personal preferences and aspirations are supressed in favor of a common survival drive. If the sense of crisis persists long enough, the organization gradually develops a new action potential compatible with the new thrust. But cultural adaptation is a long process (three to six years for a reasonably sized ESO). Frequently, the sense of crisis dissipates long before the cultural transformation is complete. Also frequently, management which was originally vigorous in enforcing the new behavior, either gets tired of acting as a policeman or turns its attention to other priority concerns.

It is at this point that historical perferences begin to reassert themselves. Forces within the organization begin to reverse the changes which are out of line with the historical culture and tradition. One common example is found in business firms where strategic planning, originally installed with noise and fanfare by the top management, quietly regresses several years later to extrapolative long-range planning.

Definition: Strategic Drift is a slow, organic and unguided transition of the strategic thrust and strategic action potential to another level.

Strategic shift is also observable during a slow shift in the internal power balance. In a dramatic power shift the new controlling management is likely to assert itself through rapid and guided realignment of the thrust. But when the power shift is gradual, strategic drift is more likely. A particular unit may gradually acquire power, either because it is emerging as the key to the success of the ESO, or because it accumulates more than its share of resources, or because its management is skillful in the use of manipulation of power. The unit uses this power to force the ESO towards its own preferred strategic thrust.

Since the psychological preferences of the majority of individuals are for stability and low risk, the drift will frequently be toward a change-resisting culture and thrust. This is the case in most non-profit ESOs. In manufacturing-intensive firms, the tendency is frequently the same, because the natural culture of manufacturing is the stable/reactive. But a drift may also be in a positive direction. This occurred in the 1930s when the marketing culture began to overcome the earlier dominance by manufacturing. In firms in which the power balance shifts to R & D a similar positive shift will occur.

Yet another and increasingly important source of drift is management technology. As discussed earlier, ESOs, and business firms in particular, are increasingly adopting new management techniques and approaches. the adoption may be the act of well-educated and perceptive management, or it may be an imitation of what 'everybody else is doing'. If the newly adopted technique is supported by management long enough to survive the resistance and to become institutionalized, it will begin to force adaptation of the culture and other elements of the action potential. This was the sense of Winston Churchill's remark which we quoted at the head of Chapter 6: 'First we shape our structures, and afterwards they shape us.'

HYPOTHESIS 11.7: STRATEGIC DRIFT

Strategic drift may occur under the following conditions:
1. When the pressure which had previously forced a change in the strategic thrust is lifted prematurely;
2. When the power balance shifts, not enough to give one group a clear dominance, but sufficiently to enable it to force a drift towards its own culture;
3. When a change in the managerial structure or systems gradually brings about cultural change;
4. Organizational drift is most likely to occur in ESOs with distributed power.

12 Model of Transition Behavior

'The only way to predict the future is to have the power over the future'

Eric Hofer

'To be or not to be. That is the question!'

Shakespeare

MODES OF TRANSITION

In earlier chapters we have identified five levels of strategic behavior: stable, reactive, anticipating, exploring and creative. In the preceding chapter we identified three modes of behavior within or across these levels:

1. *In budgeting behavior* an ESO confines itself to progressive non-dramatic changes in the allocation and size of its budgets.
2. *In strategically adaptive behavior* an ESO may make dramatic reallocation and expansions/contractions of the budgets, as well as incremental changes in products, markets, technology, or in its managerial capability, or in logistic capability. But all of the changes are consistent with the historical culture of the ESO.
3. *In strategically discontinuous* behavior an ESO makes a shift in the strategic thrust, or in the strategic action potential, or both. The behavior is discontinuous, contrary to the norms of the historical culture of the ESO.

All three modes of behavior are dealt with in the literature of several disciplines, but usually one at a time. We have brought

196

Figure 12.1   Multidisciplinary Description of Behavior Roles

Behavior Mode Chandler's Classification	Strategic Discontinuity	Strategic Adaptation	Budgeting
Strategy	Shift in level of strategic thrust Focus on Strategy Novel patterns of decisions Entrepreneurship	Changes consistent with historical thrust Focus on Competition Familiar pattern of decisions Innovation	Changes confined to budgeting Focus on Operations No visible strategic decisions Competition
Structure	Shift in culture and in strategic action potential Novel programs Cognitive Discontinuity New Models of Reality Novel Production Functions	Intraculture adaptation in strategic action potential New mix of Familiar Programs Cognitive Adaptation Adaptation of Prior Model of Reality Adaptation of Production Function	Expansion/Contraction of historical strategic action potential Re-programming Familiar Mix Cognitive Stability Fixed Model of Reality Fixed Production Function

them together into a common framework in Figure 12.1. Each mode is described in several different ways, using languages found in disparate disciplines.

In the left-hand column the terminology is that of Chandler, who lumps the modes of external strategic behavior under the word 'strategy' and the strategic action potential under 'structure'. The descriptions of the respective modes in the first lines of 'strategy' and 'structure' are in the language of this book. The second line for strategy is found in the strategic planning literature. The third is from Henry Mintzberg, who introduced the concept of strategy as a pattern of decisions made by a firm. In the last line we use microeconomic terminology. In the description of structure the second line is adapted from Simon and March; the third line is from social psychology; the fourth from organizational sociology; and the last from microeconomics.

The preceding discussion has shown that when a strategic shift occurs through a gradual drift the strategic thrust and the strategic action potential remain more or less balanced. However, when the shift is rapid the two get out of alignment. This affects the ESO in two important ways:

(1) the strategic effectiveness potential is reduced; and (2) the organizational transition becomes turbulent and inefficient. Therefore, an important characteristic which determines the effectiveness of a strategic shift is the *alignment* of an ESO during the process. In preceding chapters, we have treated various elements of the alignment. In Figure 12.2 we have gathered all of these elements. As the figure demonstrates, the alignment is more complex than a simple match between strategy and structure. Five elements are involved: environmental turbulence, strategic thrust, culture, managerial capability and logistic capability.

State *A* in the figure illustrates an ESO which has previously adapted itself to the environment. State *B* illustrates the same ESO after a change in turbulence has produced a rapid accommodation in the strategic thrust but strategic potential has not yet followed. State *B* is unstable: if support of the new thrust is withdrawn or relaxed prematurely, the ESO will drift back to state *A*. If strategic leadership continues to maintain the thrust at *B*, strategic action potential will change gradually to state *B*.

As discussed previously, one option open to management for expediting a transition of the strategic action potential (but not necessarily for reducing the inertial resistance) is to force a

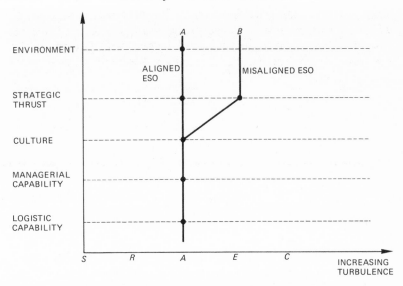

Figure 12.2   Alignment of Strategic Behavior

simultaneous rapid shift in both the strategic thrust and the management system supporting it (by introducing, for example, a strategic planning system). A less disruptive but a longer-lasting change option is through a gradual organizational learning process.

HYPOTHESIS 12.1: EFFECTIVENESS OF STRATEGIC SHIFT

A strategic shift which preserves the· alignment of thrust and strategic action potential will be more efficient and the result more stable than a shift accompanied by major misalignments.

TRANSITION TRIGGERS

On some occasions (particularly when top management is rapidly replaced, or a crisis strikes) a strategic shift occurs suddenly and dramatically. On other occasions, as our discussion of lag response has shown, there is a sequential progression from budgeting to strategic adaptation to strategic shift. We had previously defined the point of shift from budgeting to strategic adaptation as the *aspiration trigger*. We now label the point at which a strategic shift is started as the *strategic trigger*. A special case of the strategic trigger is a *crisis trigger*, which occurs in the midst of a survival crisis. We have demonstrated the three triggers in graphic form in Figure 12.3.

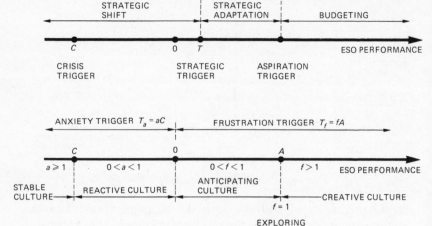

Figure 12.3   Transition Triggers

As discussed earlier in detail, the aspiration trigger correlates with the culture of an ESO. Active cultures strive for high performance levels, change-resisting ones satisfice. The strategic trigger is similarly affected by culture in the manner shown in the lower part of Figure 12.3. The figure shows that the strategic trigger may have two different origins. The first is a frustration with failure to reach performance aspirations through either budgeting or strategically adaptive behavior. We can relate this *strategic frustration trigger* T_f to the aspiration trigger by the expression:

$$T_f = fA,$$

where f is the *frustration coefficient*. As the lower part of the figure shows, the strategic frustration trigger occurs at positive performance levels. The ESO is not losing any money but it is dissatisfied with the amount it makes. The figure shows that creative ESOs actively search for opportunities to make a strategic shift. These are firms which upset the environment by escalating its level of turbulence. They do not wait for the aspiration trigger to occur ($f>1$). The exploring ESOs are open to thrust changes but do not seek it. Once the aspiration trigger is reached, they react without delay ($f = 1$). Anticipating ESOs, on the other hand, will fist try to return to the aspiration level through strategic adaptation ($0<f<1$). However, they do not tolerate losses and will take a shift before losses occur.

In stable and reactive cultures a strategic trigger occurs not from frustration with inadequate performance, but from fear of crisis. We shall call this the *anxiety trigger* ($T_a = aC$). As the figure shows, reactive cultures are generally triggered by prospects of a crisis, but stable cultures need to be hit by an actual crisis before they resort to a strategic shift.

Both frustrations and anxieties are translated into action through power. Until a 'critical power mass' sufficient to trigger the shift is reached, the frustrations and anxiety cumulate, affect morale and reduce organizational efficiency. The strategic trigger occurs either when the group or groups in power perceive a shift to be desirable, or becomes necessary when a power shift enables a new, previously powerless group to impose its strategic preferences on the ESO.

A change in preferences may be triggered by several conditions:
1. Occurrence of a crisis;
2. A shift in the level of environmental turbulence;
3. Introduction of a new system which alters the ESOs perception of its environment.

Power shifts may occur:

1. When the new management is promoted to replace a retiring group;
2. When external stakeholders force a change of key managers;
3. When a unit of the ESO which has gradually accumulated power at the expense of others (through political maneuvering, through accumulation of key resources or knowledge)

reaches a position from which it can affect a *de facto* takeover of power;
4. When a similar takeover occurs because a unit has become critical to the success of the ESO (e.g. takeover of power by marketing from production).

HYPOTHESIS 12.2: CAUSE OF STRATEGIC TRIGGER
Creative, exploring and anticipatory ESOs shift to strategically discontinuous behavior as a result of frustration with the outcomes produced by strategic adaptation. The stable and reactive ESOs are triggered by fear of crisis.

HYPOTHESIS 12.3: MECHANISM OF STRATEGIC TRIGGER
A strategic trigger will occur either when there is a pervading sense of crisis within the ESO, or when a coalition within the ESO is convinced of the need for a shift and has sufficient power to influence the rest of the ESO.

PATTERNS OF TRANSITION

Several typical transition patterns are summarized in Figure 12.4. The tables at the left-hand side of the figure show three distinctive sequences. In the first sequence the initial reaction to the aspiration trigger is introverted, focused on internal adaptation; in the second the ESOs first response is extroverted, directed toward the market; the third sequence shows the most rational ESO, which chooses a response that is appropriate to the situation.

Shown at the right of Figure 12.4 are the conditions that are likely to lead to the choice of a particular sequence. These are the configuration of power, culture, and strategic leadership.

The key question in the timing of response is whether an ESO experiences a strategic trigger early enough to make an orderly transition, or whether it will have to pay the penalities of an emergency shift under crisis. In Chapter 5 we have shown that the answer to this question depends, first, on the novelty of the threatening event, and second, on the speed with which it develops.

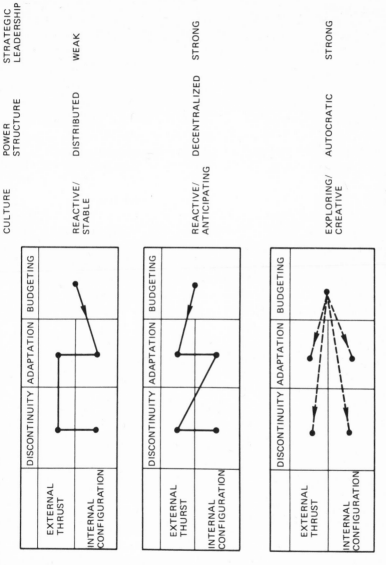

Figure 12.4 Patterns of Transition Behavior

Definition: The speed of an environmental disturbance is reciprocal of the time period between the moment of the aspiration trigger and the moment of full impact on the ESO.

Thus $S = \dfrac{1}{T_{AS}}$, where S is the speed and T_{AS} is the time period.

Using the results of the preceding chapter, we have constructed in Figure 12.5 the sequence and timing of a typical response by a stable culture. The figure also applies to reactive ESOs with weak leadership. Two time periods are identified for each stage of response: above the dashed line is the time needed for managerial decision-making, and below is the time needed for implementing the selected measures.

In accordance with our previous discussion, a stable/reactive ESO does not turn its attention to a new environmental disturbance until after the aspiration level has been pierced. This produces a delay Δ_1. Delays Δ_2 and Δ_3 are incurred in the process of selecting and implementing the retrenchment measures. Reference back to Figure 6.2 reminds us that stable/reactive ESOs are plodding problem solvers: measures are selected and tried sequentially until a satisfactory result is achieved. This is indicated by the double feedback arrows in Figure 12.5. After the retrenchment measures such ESOs will usually try incremental strategic changes, adding delays Δ_4 and Δ_5.

As previously discussed, the strategic trigger may or may not occur in time for an orderly shift to a new level of behavior. This will depend, on the one hand, on the amount of time remaining before the environmental disturbance makes its full impact on the ESO, and, on the other hand, on the time required to carry out an orderly response. If we represent the times necessary for orderly managerial and logistic shifts by Δ_6 and Δ_7, we can express the condition which permits an orderly shift by the inequality:

$$T_{AS} - (\Delta_L + \Delta_2 + \Delta_3 + \Delta_4 + \Delta_5) > \Delta_6 + \Delta_7$$

If the inequality does not hold, an emergency crisis-like response is needed. It should be recalled, however, that stable/reactive ESOs are typically myopic. At the outset they may not perceive that the above inequality does not hold and that a

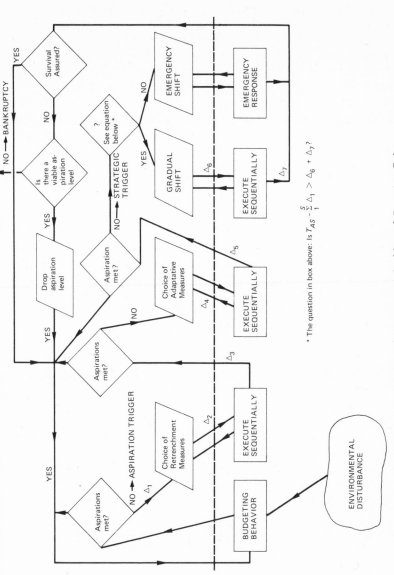

Figure 12.5 Timing of Response in Stable and Reactive Cultures

* The question in box above: Is $T_{AS} - \sum_{1}^{S} \Delta_1 > \Delta_6 + \Delta_7$?

crisis is imminent. Gradual shift will be initiated first and continued until a crisis breaks out, at which time the gradual shift is suddenly transformed into an extreme emergency.

The upper right-hand part of Figure 12.5 calls attention to the fact that, for reasons discussed in the preceding chapter, survival is not assured and a possible outcome for the shift activity is bankruptcy. Another outcome is restoration of performance to the level of aspiration. If the impact of the environmental disturbance is not fully reversible, but not fatal to the ESO, a third outcome may be to stabilize performance at a reduced level of aspiration. The reader is invited to trace the sequence of events in these three outcomes by following the computer-like logic of the upper right-hand part of Figure 12.5.

In Figure 12.6 we present the timing of response for anticipating ESOs and for a subclass of reactive ESOs which have strong and vigorous strategic leadership. The latter are exemplified by large firms in oligopolistic industries, such as the automotive or chemicals. For the anticipative ESO the aspiration trigger occurs $-\Delta_1$ ahead of an actual decline in performance. In such ESOs, forecasting is a part of a larger planning system which selects an optimal mix of measures. Instead of the one-at-a-time sequential work of stable ESOs, anticipating ESOs undertake a coordinated program of measures. As a result, trial and error is eliminated and the time Δ_2 is shorter than the corresponding period in a stable ESO.

However, when a strategic trigger occurs, these ESOs find themselves captives of their own culture and capability. While competent in dealing with incremental intracultural changes, they have no more competence for dealing with novel phenomena than the stable/reactive ESO. They are even likely to require a longer time for the shift decision (Δ_4) than do the stable ESOs (Δ_6 in Figure 12.5), the reason being their confidence that the existing planning system can solve all important problems. While the ESO persists in this 'I know how to do it' mode, valuable time is lost during which outside competence could be called in or new decision-making capabilities could be developed.

However, even with this delay, an anticipating ESO has a better chance for an orderly strategic shift and a better chance for survival: first, because it anticipates the future; secondly, because its intracultural strategic responses are more efficient; and thirdly, because it uses fewer steps to arrive at a shift. Thus an orderly shift

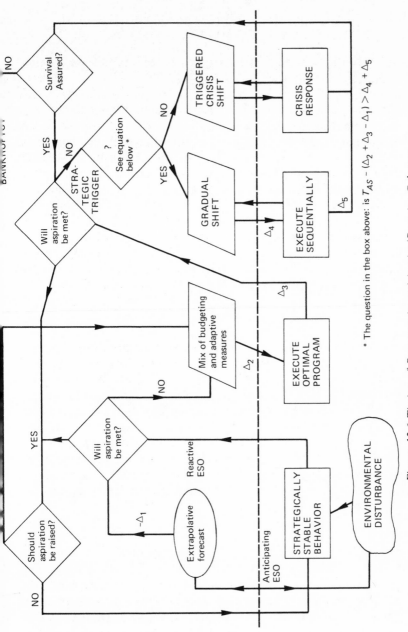

Figure 12.6 Timing of Response in anticipation/Reactive Cultures

* The question in the box above: is $T_{AS} - (\Delta_2 + \Delta_3 - \Delta_1) > \Delta_4 + \Delta_5$

is possible if the following inequality holds:

$$(T_{AS} + \Delta_1) - (\Delta_2 + \Delta_3) > \Delta_4 + \Delta_5$$

in which the forecast time horizon Δ_1 is seen to increase the time available for response.

Figure 12.7, the last of a series of three, shows the timing for exploring and creative ESOs. Environmental surveillance now supplements extrapolative forecasting in two important ways: by extending the time horizon for identification of significant disturbances, thus increasing Δ_1, and by capturing in advance many environmental disturbances which become evident in other cultures only after their ultimate impact on the performance.

As the figure shows, exploring and creative ESOs have the cultural openness and technical sophistication to treat stable, adaptive and discontinuous responses as a set of alternatives. From this set they select an appropriate mix of measures and implement them in parallel streams. The result is a further improvement in timing. The inequality now becomes:

$$T_{AS} + \Delta_1 > \Delta_2 + \Delta_3$$

This means that when an environmental disturbance requires a strategic shift, an exploring/creative ESO will respond directly, without preliminary effort to find a solution through adaptive measures.

As the figure shows, creative/exploring ESOs continually re-examine their aspirations. If the outcome of the shift programs does not come up to the expectations, the environmental surveillance is intensified in search for new alternatives. If the programs meet or exceed the previously estalished aspirations, the aspirations are revised upward and new programs are launched.

SUMMARY MODEL OF TRANSITION BEHAVIOR

In Figure 12.4, we have explored the sequences of attention to the external thrust and internal action potential as a function of particular combinations of culture, power and strategic leadership. In Figures 12.5, 12.6 and 12.7, we introduced the speed of

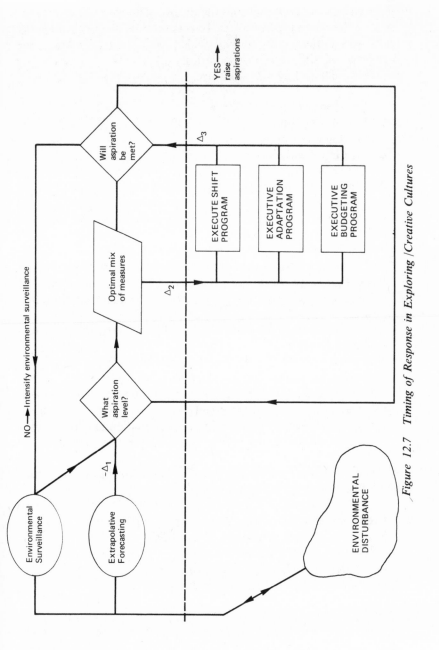

Figure 12.7 Timing of Response in Exploring /Creative Cultures

the environmental change and the timing of strategic response for each of the three typical cases. In this section, we generalize the transition behavior in a way which permits us to trace the outcome of different combinations of the key determining variables. These key variables are:

1. Environmental turbulence
2. Power structure
3. Strategic culture
4. Strategic leadership
5. ESO resources
6. Managerial and logistic capabilities.

To keep the number of combinations manageable, we limit the values which each can assume:

The environment is either in the stable condition (requiring the budgeting response mode), or on one of the higher levels of turbulence requiring strategic adaptation, or in a transition to a new level of turbulence;
The culture within the ESO is either change-seeking or change-resisting;
The power is either centralized or distributed;
The strategic leadership is either weak or strong;
The resources of the ESO are either adequate or not adequate to support a given strategic shift;
The capabilities are either adequate or inadequate to effect a transition of the thrust before the ESO goes bankrupt.

We have summarized all the possible response paths in Figure 12.8. The following notation is used:

Free-form shapes represent environmental inputs;
Square boxes are attributes of the ESO;
Circles describe political behavior;
Ovals describe strategic behavior;
Diamonds stand for triggering events.

We can start exploring the figure with concentric circles labelled (2) in the lower left-hand corner. It denotes continuous and ongoing power struggle within the ESO. As a result of the power struggle or of a political input from the environment (1), a power shift (3) may occur in which power is transferred to a new group (5) or individual. If the strategic action culture (4) of the new power structure is the same as of the preceding one, the new leaders will not be motivated to change the strategic behavior unless the ESO is failing to meet its aspirations. On the other hand, if the strategic outlook of the new leadership is different, it will be inclined to change the strategic behavior of the ESO *even if there is no stimulus from the environment for doing so.*

Whether this inclination is translated into actuality depends on the strength of the leadership within the new power structure (5). If the leadership is strong the proverbial 'new broom will sweep clean' and the ESO will go through a strategic discontinuity (6). If the leadership is weak the most it will do will be to challenge and change the previous level of the ESOs aspirations (14).

In the former case a strategic shift triggered by a takeover of power will not necessarily be beneficial to the ESO nor even guarantee its survival. For example, if the power shift is occasioned by a failure of the previous management to cope with increased environmental turbulence, a new conservative group may reinforce a return of behavior to the 'good old times' appropriate to the earlier turbulence era, thus further imperilling the chances of survival. In another example, a group of 'hot-head' entrepreneurs may take over management of a stable, solid but unexciting firm and squander its resources and capabilities on wild diversification and acquisition schemes.

If the new power structure impels the ESO toward a better alignment with the environment, the outcome will depend on the size of the strategic gap, the characteristics of the environment, and the ESOs resources and capabilities. We shall discuss the alternative outcomes presently.

Returning to step (1), the environmental change may not be a political one but rather a commercial or a subsidy change. As the figure shows, the response will depend on whether the power structure is centralized or distributed. If power is distributed, the disturbance will not be recognized until after the aspiration trigger (step 14). If power is centralized, further progress is determined by whether the dominant culture (13) is change-seeking or change-resisting. In the latter case the environmental change will again be recognized only after the aspiration trigger (14). In the former case the response will be further determined by the quality of strategic leadership (15) within the dominant culture. Weak leadership will procrastinate until the aspiration trigger (14). But strong, change-seeking leadership will survey the environment and diagnose whether the environmental disturbance calls for a strategic shift. If the answer is yes, the management will trigger a strategic shift program without delay (6). If the disturbance is perceived as controllable by measures short of the shift, management will trigger an appropriate mode of behavior: either budgeting activity (17) or strategic adaptation (18).

Thus a number of alternative paths lead to box 14 in which the response is determined by the differences between ESO performance and the aspirations. If the performance remains above aspirations, the ESO will persist in strategically stable budgeting behavior (17), although the intensity of the behavior may increase as the performance gap widens.

As we discussed earlier, the trigger to the next step (exit NO from box 19) occurs after a procrastination time delay. At this point, the ESO increasingly engages in strategic adaptation (18). If the environmental disturbance which originally triggered the activities can be treated by strategic adaptation, the measures will be successful and the ESO will return to the budgeting behavior.

If the measures are not successful, the ESO will persist until it becomes evident that adaptation will not help and that a strategic discontinuity must be confronted (21). When this occurs, a search starts for the 'savior group' (22) with a strong leadership potential (26) and for relevant capability (23). The result of the search is either an internal transfer of power (27) or acquisition of new leadership (24) and competence (25) from the outside.

Following the political shift, the new leadership turns to the strategic shift. Its success, in the first place, depends on the correctness of its diagnosis. If it misperceives the problem, it will propel the ESO on its way to bankruptcy (7). If the problem is perceived correctly, the ability of the ESO to cope with it will depend *whether there is a solution* in the environment (28). If the environment has become a strategic trap, bankruptcy is again inevitable. If solution is possible, the adequacy of the ESOs resources (8), the gap in the capability that needs to be closed (9), and the speed of the environmental change relative to the ESOs response (10) — all three of these factors will determine whether the ESO can adapt or not. If an adaptation occurs, as the completion of the strategic shift the ESO will revert to budgeting behavior if its dominant culture is change-resisting, or to strategic adaptation behavior if the culture is change-seeking (29).

We now summarize the somewhat complex Figure 12.8 by means of the key propositions which have been advanced:

HYPOTHESIS 12.4: FORCES AFFECTING TRANSITION BEHAVIOR

1. An ESO will persist either in budgeting or strategic adaptation behavior until an aspiration trigger whenever one or more of the following conditions is present:
   a. The dominant culture is change-resisting;
   b. Power is distributed;
   c. Strategic leadership is weak.
2. Following an aspiration trigger, such ESOs will follow a sequential pattern of transition behavior: from budgeting to strategic adaptation to strategic discontinuity for stable ESOs and from strategic adaptation to strategic discontinuity for other cultures.
3. Under the above pattern, the shift to discontinous behavior is typically preceded by a transfer of power to new management.
4. Discontinuous behavior may be triggered by:
   a. Strong, change-seeking strategic leadership which perceives a change in the environmental turbulence;
   b. Failure by the ESO to reverse a negative trend through budgeting adaptive behavior;
   c. Strong new management which seeks to impose its strategic culture on the ESO, regardless of environmental implications.
5. Strategically discontinuous behavior will succeed if:
   a. The environmental turbulence shift has not transformed the industry into a strategic trap;
   b. The ESO has the necessary resources to invest in the strategic shift;
   c. If its capability gap is bridgeable in time to avert a destructive impact of the environmental disturbance. Failing any of the above conditions, the ESO will fail.

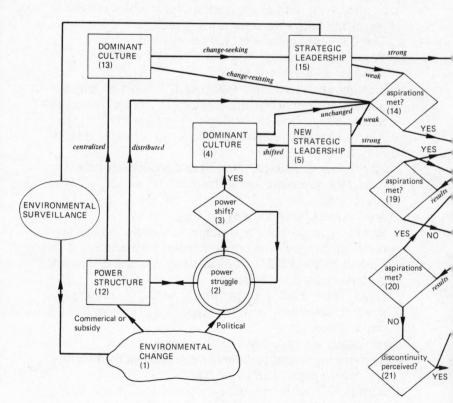

Figure 12.8   Impact of: Environment, Power, Leadership, Culture on Transition Behavior

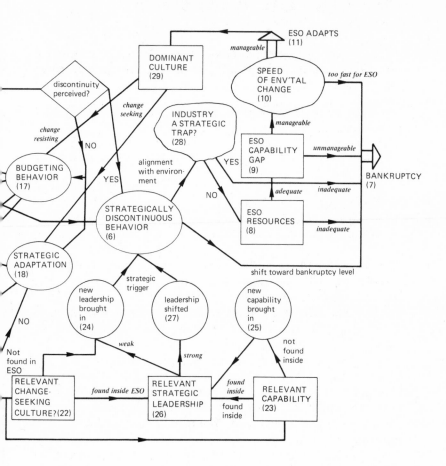

13 The Basic Axioms

'The real importance of the Greeks for the progress of the world is that they discovered the almost incredible secret that speculative reason was itself subject to orderly method.'

'I now state the thesis that the explanation of . . . active attack on the environment is a three-fold urge: (i) to live, (ii) to live well, (iii) to live better. In fact the art of life is *first* to be alive, *secondly*, to be alive in a satisfactory way, and *thirdly*, to acquire an increase in satisfaction.'

Alfred North Whitehead

EPISTEMOLOGY OF COMPLEXITY

This book is, above all, an exercise in the comprehension of complexity. All individuals who call themselves scientists are united by a common drive to perceive order in reality and to capture this perception in ways which increases human understanding of the awesome complexity which management academics call 'the real world'.

One time-honored approach to comprehending the real world is to identify within it phenomena which match the particular scientific optic of the observing scientist. Thus psychologists seek problems which can be explained through variables of personal and inter-personal behavior, political scientists focus on the phenomenon of power.

Such differentiation of scientific optics has been pioneered and elaborated by students of the 'natural' (as opposed to the 'social') world. A result of this elaboration has been a progressive subdivision of science into compartmentalized disciplines. During the past three hundred years the scientific archetype of a generalist-philosopher has been replaced by that of an increasingly specialised physicist, chemist or biologist.

216

Another result has been the development of the *scientific method*. This method is an empirical heuristic which holds that the truth or untruth of any assertion about the real world is established only through a process of experimental verification. This empirical validation heuristic has proved to be a powerful tool in enabling mankind to understand and master the world of natural phenomena. But it has also contributed to a further narrowing of the 'slice' of complexity which is studied at any given time. To be of interest to an empirical scientist, not only must the problem be homeomorphic with his scientific equipment but it must also be *empirically testable*.

During the twentieth century the social science – economics, psychology and to a smaller extent sociology and political science – began to adapt the empirical heuristic and, with it, the methodology of partitioning the real world into slices of manageable complexity. Today a majority of scientists, both natural and social, are practitioners of this methodology.

Complexity-partitioning has worked magnificently whenever the variables included in the optic of the scientist are also the variables which are determinant in the slice of reality under study. The method has repeatedly failed whenever one or both of the following conditions occurred: (1) the 'slice' was not sufficiently self-contained, so that behavior within it was just as influenced by the surrounding variables as by the variables inside the slice; and (2) the scientist's optic did not match (was not homeomorphic in the language of mathematics) with the critical internal variables. Thus, for example, psychology fails to explain behavior in situations in which, in addition to personal and interpersonal affect, the phenomenon of power plays a dominant role.

Another way of expressing this is to say that complexity-partitioning is a case of an explanation in search of a problem. When the two match the approach works, when they are mismatched the result is, at best, an imcomplete and, at worst, a false understanding of reality.

A second, and at the present time more fundamental, shortcoming is that the selection of the problems to be treated follows the logic of science and not the logic of society's priorities. Until after World War Two this discrepancy has not been a problem. In the first place the real world was itself subdivided in 'slices'; it was structured, stable, compartmentalized. In the second place the contributions of science were a bonus which improved solutions to problems which society had already solved through natural evolution.

Since World War Two society has become progressively turbulent and interconnected, and its problems complex and multidisciplinary. Many of these problems remain unsolved. Scientific knowledge has become one of the major social forces which determine whether the present civilization will survive or die. As a result, partitioning of complexity has become less and less responsive to society's needs today. The response of the scientific community falls into several categories.

One substantial majority believes (and often with justification) that there are still many exciting and socially beneficial scientific horizons to be conquered within the limits of scientific disciplines. This group leaves the worry about social priorities to non-scientists and politicians.

Another category of scientists is concerned about society's priorities but believes that 'one cannot build a house until all the bricks are made'. This category also typically believes that treatment of complexity is simply additive. First, all of the elements must be explored through complexity-partitioning. Once this is done, problems of high complexity can be treated by straightforward combination. Thus the shape of a house becomes evident once the necessary bricks have been fabricated and put on inspection.

Both of the above categories persist in partitioning of complexity. However, a third and growing group of scientists holds, on the one hand, that integration of compartmentalized knowledge is not simply additive and, on the other, that design of houses need not, indeed must not, be delayed until all the bricks are made. They hold that complex problems have important *systemic* properties (such as, for example, the organizing principle of a complex set of elements). This category concerns itself with varying approaches to *synthesis of complexity*.

This concern starts with a recognition that complexity reduction is not capricious narrow-mindedness. Rather, it reflects a recognition that the complexity of the real world is many times greater than the complexity-handling capacity of the human brain. Therefore, synthesis of complexity must compensate for the bounded rationality of the human mind.

One currently widely used method for doing this goes under the name of the *systems approach*, the computerized version of which is known as *simulation*. Both build large and complex models of the world out of elementary complexity slices. The method is laborious, time-consuming, impressive in the volume of information it handles and the complexity it encompasses. But conceptually it is very simple, and adds but one additional ingredient to the unidisciplinary inquiry.

Rather than use simple addition, the systems approach focuses on the nature of *linkages* and *interrelationships* between *mutually adjacent* slices of reality. Groups of adjacent slices are next connected to other groups, thus making possible a structure of an arbitrary degree of complexity. A key feature in the method is that the analyst is not required to (and cannot) comprehend the total complexity. He only needs to understand the slices and the adjacent interrelationships.

Prior to the electronic computer the practical limits on complexity synthesis were imposed by the computational technology. In many cases exploration of a complex model of reality required more time than was necessary to conduct an experimental test, or even to allow the real system to find its own solution through trial and error. But electronic computers have changed all this. The complexity-handling capacity of the computer is rapid and virtually unlimited. The practical limits are imposed by the costs and the time required to build the model and, particularly, by the availability of the necessary data.

Typically, the complexity embodied in a systems analysis or in a simulation far exceeds the comprehension of the scientists who constructed it. When a simulation model is completed, the builders have a right to claim that they have built a mirror image of a complex reality. *But they are typically unable to describe the image in words and concepts that explain its complexity.* Instead the builders 'run' the simulation: they postulate values of certain key ('independent') variables and the computer model predicts the values of other important ('dependent') variables. Thus, in engineering terms, a simulation is a large 'black box' which relates 'inputs' to 'outputs'.

Another method for synthesizing complexity was invented by the Greeks and brilliantly illustrated by the great Greek philosopher-mathematician Euclid some 2200 years ago. This illustration is found in a body of mathematics which today is known as Euclidian geometry. Instead of replacing human rationality by the computer model, Euclid uses *complexity aggregation* (or complexity compression) to overcome the bounds of human rationality. The method is based on the assumption that in all very complex situations it is possible to identify a small number of relatively simple explanations ('axioms' in Euclid's language) which have two properties: (1) they explain complexity at the highest level; and (2) explanations of lower levels of complexity can be derived from the higher levels by logical inference.

Some 2100 years after Euclid, the manager-philosopher Chester Barnard arrived at a very similar conclusion that, no matter how complex a managerial problem, it is usually possible to identify a small number of *strategic variables* which determine the essential shape of the solution.

The Euclidian method is essentially a hierarchical one. At the top is a very high level complexity which offers a highly concise explanation for everything that occurs at lower levels. (A brilliant modern example is Einstein's formula $E = mc^2$, which contains within it all relationships between energy and physical mass.) The method also specifies rules of deduction, or logic, which can be used both to derive and test explanations on progressively partitioned levels of complexity.

This method which, for purposes of comparison to other ways of handling complexity, we have called the method of complexity aggregation is popularly known as *theory-building*. It flourished under the Greeks, languished during the Middle Ages, and was revived by the Renaissance philosopher-scientists. It remained a dominant method of search for knowledge until the early twentieth century. Its glorious achievements are represented by such supreme practitioners as Leonardo da Vinci, Galileo, Newton, Maxwell, Mendeleef, Darwin, Bohr, and Einstein. During the twentieth century, complexity-partitioning has progressively replaced theory-building as the dominant method of scientific inquiry. Today, theory-builders remain dominant only in mathematics, which is an essentially non-empirical science. In all other fields, including philosophy, empirically-based complexity-partitioning is the central theme.

There is a popular misconception that theory-building proceeds in a deductive manner, that lower-level insights follow the aggregate insight. In fact, in all important historical applications the method proceeded in the other direction, from particular insights to the ultimate generalization. But neither is the method a mechanistically inductive one. The ultimate generalization is typically a flash of genius, an integrative insight by the subconscious processes of the scientist, which suddenly reveals to his conscious self a basic order in a sea of previously incomprehensible complexity. The logical relationships with the lower order of complexity are derived later, partly to derive new low-level understandings and partly to test the validity of the ultimate insight. Thus theory building is both inductive, because the ultimate insight is born of lower-level experiences, and deductive, because this insight enriches the partitioned complexity.

Like all others, the method of complexity compression has its shortcomings. Because of the need to compress the explanations into a form comprehensible to the human mind, it tends to give a more simplified picture of reality than does either complexity-partitioning or the systems approach. At the highest level it gives only an aggregate 'strategic' view of the system behavior without the richness of detail available from simulation. But it gives a comprehensible view of high complexity and captures the systematic properties which belong to that level.

It should be clear from the preceding discussion that the three major historical methods for comprehension of complexity are not substitutes for each other, but are, rather, complementary alternative optics which yield different explanations of reality. The compression of complexity was invented over two thousand years ago, the partitioning of complexity evolved within the last three hundred years, and the systems method within the last hundred. As mentioned before, today a majority of scientists practice complexity-partitioning and the values and the culture of this knowledge heuristic dominate scientific thought. Social priorities, on the other hand, demand increasing use of complexity-synthesizing methods.

As mentioned before, one of the cornerstones of complexity-partitioning is the empirical validation heuristic. During the past hundred years this heuristic has been incorporated into theory-building. The typical approach is to derive from the basic axioms a simple, experimentally testable statement and then validate the statement through an experiment. The classic historical examples are the Michelson-Morley experiments, and the 'red-shift' experiment conducted to test the validity of Einstein's generalizations.

The key features of such experiments is that they convert a generalized statement (such as Einstein's relativity equations) into computable and measurable outcomes (such as differences in the time of light propagation under two different conditions). Herein lies both the strength and the weakness of empirical validation. If such unambiguous conversion can be made, a limited experiment validates an enormously comprehensive theory. But if the quantitative inference is not possible, there is no way (within the empirical heuristic) to tell whether the theory is true or not. This condition is typical of most social-behavior theories. In the absence of possible empirical tests, they typically remain personal hypotheses advanced by different scientists. As a result, the word 'theory' has acquired a slightly pejorative connotation, synonymous with 'speculation' and invoking 'impractical' as a necessary adjective.

The marriage of the Euclidian complexity compression and of the Galilean empirical validation strengthened the natural sciences and weakened the social sciences. Further, the dominance of empiricism has obscured the fact that the original complexity compression methodology invented by the Greeks had its own well-developed (non-empirical) methodology for testing the validity of a theory. In *The Function of Reason*, written in 1929, Alfred North Whitehead called this dominance of empiricism 'a colossal example of anti-empirical dogmatism'. He also re-stated the validation heuristic which had been in use for two thousand years before Galileo first dropped objects from the tower of Pisa. In his words:

> The Greek logic as finally perfected by the experience of centuries provides a set of criteria to which the content of a belief should be subjected. These are:
> 1. Conformity to intuitive experience;
> 2. Clarity of the propositional content;
> 3. Internal logical consistency;
> 4. External logical consistency;
> 5. Status of a logical scheme with:
>   a. widespread conformity to experience;
>   b. no discordance with experience;
>   c. coherence among its categorical notions;
>   d. methodological consequences.

As the patient reader of this book has undoubtedly observed, this book is written in the axiomatic Euclidian tradition. The purpose of this section has been twofold: first, to identify this book with a great, but currently neglected tradition of human inquiry; secondly, to offer the reader Whitehead's criteria by which the validity of the hypotheses offered in this book can be evaluated. It now remains to bring together the central axioms of this book.

KEY AXIOMS

Like most efforts at theory-building, the eight years of preparation and two years of writing that have gone into this book have proceeded both inductively and deductively. The key axioms did not become visible until the late stages. It is appropriate, therefore, to place them at the end, rather than at the beginning of the book.

The axioms are about behavior of environment-dependent and environment-serving organizations in complex and turbulent environment. Both as a mnemonic device and as a means of paying tribute to the individuals who had a major influence on this book, we shall attach names to the respective axioms.

I Whitehead's Axiom

This axiom is about the influence of individuals on organizations. I named it after Whitehead because of my educational antecedents. Behavioral psychologists would probably name it 'Maslow's axiom'.

1. The behavior of each individual is motivated by an aspiration for security (survival) and an aspiration for achievement. Since achievement entails risk, each individual makes a personal and different trade-off between the two aspirations.
2. Individuals join and use organizations to achieve their respective security/achievement aspirations.
3. The vigour with which an individual pursues his aspirations is determined by the strength of his achievement drive and the power at his disposal (see Machiavelli's Axiom).

II *Machiavelli's Axiom*

This axiom is about power.
1. Individuals and groups seek to attain their aspirations by influencing others to behave in accordance with their preferences.
2. Their influence depends on the degree of control which they possess over allowing and/or denying other the fulfillment of their aspirations.

III *J. V. Thompson's Axiom*

This axiom is about organizational dynamics.
1. Organizations have behavior tendencies which are independent and frequently contrary to the preferences of powerful participants.
2. Organizations have recognizeable collective aspirations which are not necessarily those of powerful participants.
3. Organizations resist efforts to change their prior behavior.
4. The behavior of organizations in an environment may range between the extremes of reluctant, passive adaptation to, to agressive, creative modification of the environment.

IV *Emery-Trist Axiom*

This axiom is about the influence of the environment on organizations.
1. The environment determines the modes and conditions of behavior necessary for survival and/or achievement of organizational aspiration.

V *Chandler's Axiom*

This axiom is about organizational success and survival. The success/survival of an organization depends on a two way alignment:
a. between its behavior in the environment and the conditions for success/survival defined by the environment;
b. between its behavior and its internal configuration.

At this point in the writing, the temptation is strong to construct a chart which shows the manner in which the hypotheses developed in this book follow from the axioms. I have resisted this temptation for the following reasons:

1. Such a chart would largely duplicate what was already discussed in connection with Figure 2.1;
2. The reader deserves a respite from this long and complex book;
3. So do I;
4. If I make the chart, the temptation would be overwhelming to rewrite large parts of this book;
5. If I did rewrite, my secretary would leave me, my wife would sue for divorce, and my publisher break the contract for a much overdue book;
6. The reader who has been faithful to this point deserves a chance to make his own chart. In learning-theory terms, he will thus 'internalize' what he has read.

BRETHREN, YE WHO HAVE PERSEVERED WITH ME, I SALUTE YOUR PATIENCE!

References

Ackoff, Russell L., *Concept of Corporation Planning*, (Wiley, 1970).

Ackoff, Russell L., *On Purposeful Systems*, (Aldine, 1972).

Ackoff, Russell L., *Redesigning the Future: A Systems Approach to Societal Problems*, (Wiley, 1974).

Allison, G. T., *Essence of Decision: Explaining the Cuban Missile Crisis* (Little, Brown, 1971).

Anshen, Melvin (Ed.), *Managing the Socially Responsible Corporation* (Riverside, N. J.: Macmillan, 1974).

Ansoff, H. Igor, 'Strategies for Diversification', *Harvard Business Review*, September – October, 1957.

——'A Model for Diversification', *Management Science*, Vol. 4, July, 1958.

——'Planning for Diversification Through Merger' (with Theodore Andersen, Frank Norton, and J. Fred Weston), *California Management Review*, Vol. 1, No. 4, Summer 1959.

——'A Quasi-Analytic Method for Long Range Planning.' Paper presented at the 1st Symposium on Corporate Long Range Planning, the Institute of Management Sciences, College on planning, 6 June 1959, and at the 6th Annual International Meeting, the Institute of Management Sciences, Paris, 9 September 1959.

——'Merger Objectives and Organization Structure' (with J. Fred Weston), *Review of Economics and Business*, August 1962.

——'Management Participation in Diversification'. Paper presented at Stanford Research Institute, Newark, N. J., 25 September 1963. Published in Proceedings of Client Conference, Menlo Park, California, Long Range Planning Service, Stanford Research Institute, 1963.

——'Planning as a Practical Management Tool', *Financial Executive*, June 1964.

——'A Quasi-Analytic Approach to the Business Policy Problem', *Management Technology*, Vol. 4, June 1964.

——'Company Objectives: Blueprint or Blue Sky?' *Management Review*, September 1962. Reprinted in *Management in Perspective*, (Eds., W. E. Schlender, William G. Scott and Alan C. Filley) (Houghton Mifflin, 1965).

——*Corporate Strategy* (McGraw-Hill, 1965).

——'The Firm of the Future', *Harvard Business Review*, September–October 1965.

——'Planning at the Level of an Enterprise in the USA.' Paper presented at the *2ème Congrès National de Gestion Prévisionnelle*, Paris, 14–16 September 1966. Published in the Proceedings of the Conference, Paris, 1966.

——'Research and Development Planning' (with Richard G. Brandenburg). In *Handbook of Business Administration* (Ed., H. B. Maynard) (McGraw-Hill, 1967).

——'The Expanding Role of the Computer in Managerial Decision-Making', *Informatie, Jaargang*, Amsterdam, 1967.

——'The Innovative Firm', *Enterprise: Journal of the PE Consulting Group*, July 1967.

——'Design of Optimal Business planning System: A Study Proposal' (with Richard G. Brandenburg), *Journal for Cybernetics of Planning and Organization*, March 1967.

——'The Evolution of Corporate Planning.' Report of the SRI Long Range Planning Service, Palo Alto, Calif., September 1967.

——'The General Manager of the Future' (with Richard G. Brandenburg), *California Management Review*, Vol. 2, No. 3, Spring 1969.

——'The Knowledge Professional in the Post-Industrial Era.' *Bedrijfskunde, Jaargang*, Vol. 47, No. 2, 1975, pp. 88 *ff.*

——'The State of Practice in Management Systems.' Paper presented at the 2nd U.S. – U.S.S.R. Conference on Planning, New York, May, 1975. Published as EIASM Working Paper No. 75–11. Brussels: European Institute for Advanced Studies in Management, 1975.

——'Shortcomings of Strategic Planning.' Interview in *International Management*, September 1976.

——*From Strategic Planning to Strategic Management* (Joint Ed. with Roger P. Declerck and Robert L. Hayes.) (Wiley, 1976).

——'Strategic Portfolio Management' (with James C. Leontiades), *Journal of Management*

——'Managing Surprise and Discontinuity – Strategic Response

to Weak Signals', *California Management Review*, Winter 1976.

——'Societal Strategy for the Business Firm' (with Oscar Tivis Nelson). Forthcoming.

——'The State of Practice in Planning Systems' *Sloan Management Review*, Vol. 18, No. 2, Winter 1977, pp. 1–24.

——'Strategies for a Technology-Based Business' (with John M. Stewart), *Harvard Business Review*, November–December 1967. Forthcoming in *The Managerial Mind* (Irwin).

——'An Appreciation of Industrial Dynamics' (with Dennis Slevin), *Management Science*, Vol. 14, March 1968.

——'A Language for Organizational Design' (with R. G. Brandenburg). Paper presented at OECD Working Symposium on Long Range Planning, Bellagio, Italy, October–November 1968.

——'Managerial Problem-Solving.' In *Management Science in Planning and Control* (Ed. John Blood, Jr.) (Special Technical Association Publication, No. 5. New York: The Technical Association of the Pulp and Paper Industry, 1969).

——'Vers une Théorie Stratégique des Entreprises' (Toward a Strategic Theory of the Firm), *Économies et Societés*, Tome 2, No. 3, Paris, 1968. Reprinted in English as 'Toward a Strategic Theory of the Firm' in *Business Strategy* (Ed., H. Igor Ansoff) (Penguin Books, 1969).

——'Long Range Planning in Perspective', presented at CIOS 15th Congress, Tokyo, 1969. Published in *Proceedings of the 15th CIOS International Management Congress*, Kogakusha Co. Ltd., Tokyo, 1969.

——*Business Strategy* (Ed.) (Penguin Books, 1969).

——'Toward a Strategic Theory of the Firm.' In *Business Strategy* (Ed. H. Igor Ansoff) (Penguin Books, 1969).

——'Does Planning Pay? The Effect of Planning on Success of Acquisitions in American Firms' (with Jay Anver, Richard Brandenburg, Fred Portner and Ray Radosevich), *Long Range Planning Journal*, Vol. 3, No. 2, 1970.

——'Institutional Factors in Strategic Decision-Making' (with Don Lebell), *Journal of Business Policy*, Vol. 1, No. 3, Spring 1971.

——*Acquisitions Behavior of U.S. Manufacturing Firms, 1946–65* (with Brandenburg, Richard G., Portner, F. E., and Radosevich, H. R.) (Vanderbilt University Press, 1971).

——'The Concept of Strategic Management', *Journal of Business Policy*, Vol. 2, No. 4, Summer 1972.

——'Dolgosrochnoe Planirovanic v Perspective', *Sovremennye Tendenzyi v Upravelenti v Capitalisticheskich Stranakh*, pp. 51–72 (Moscow, Izdatelstvo Progress, 1972).

——'Corporate Structure, Present and Future', *Proceedings of the Third International Conference on Corporate Planning.* (EIASM Working Paper No. 74–4, Brussels, 1973).

——'The Next Twenty Years in Management Education', *Library Quarterly*, Vol. 43, No. 4, October 1973.

——'Management in Transition' in *Challenge to Leadership: Managing in a Changing World*, pp. 22–63 (New York: Free Press, 1973).

——'Role of Models in Corporate Decision-Making' (with Robert L. Hayes). In *Systems and Management Annual, 1974* (Ed. by Russell L. Ackoff) (New York: Petrocelli Books, 1974).

——'Functions of the Executive Office in a Large Conglomerate' (EIASM Working Paper No. 85–42, Brussels, 1974).

——'Management en Advieswerk: de derde generatie', *Overdruk uit TED*, Tijdschrift voor Effectief Directiebeleid, Mei 1974.

——'La Structure de l'Entreprise Aujourd'hui et Demain', Cahier de *La Fondation Nationale Pour L'Enseignement de la Gestion*, No. 9, October 1974. Reprinted in *Chefs: Revue Suisse du Management* in two parts, February and March 1975.

——'An Applied Managerial Theory of Strategic Behavior' (EIASM Working Paper No. 75–12, Brussels, March 1975).

——(Ed.) 'Management under Discontinuity.' Proceedings of INSEAD Conference, Fontainebleau, January 1975. (EIASM Report No. 75–1.)

——'Planned Management of Turbulent Change.' Forthcoming in *McGraw-Hill Encyclopedia of General Management*.

——'Management of Strategic Surprise and Discontinuity: Problem of Managerial Decisiveness.' (EIASM Working Paper No. 29–75, Brussels, 1975).

Arrow, K. J., *General Competitive Analysis* (Holden-Day, 1971).

Ashby, W. R., *Introduction to Cybernetics*, (Wiley, 1956).

Baumol, William J., *Business Behavior, Value and Growth* (Revised Edn.), pp. 86–9, (Harcourt Brace, 1967).

Beer, Stafford, *The Brain of the Firm* (Herder and Herder, 1972). (*See* Ch. 2: Concepts and Terms; Ch. 6: Anatomy of Management.)

Bennis, W. G., *Changing Organizations* (McGraw-Hill, 1966). (*See* Ch. 7: Change Agents, Change Programs and Strategies.)

Bennis, W. G., Benne K. D., Chin R., *The Planning of Change* (2nd Edn.) (Holt, Rinehart, 1969).

Benson, J. Kenneth, 'Organization, a Dialectical View', *Administrative Science Quarterly*, Vol. 2, March 1977.

Bell, Daniel, *The Coming of Post-Industrial Society* (New York: Basic Books, 1973).

Bok, Derek C., and Dunlop, John T., *Labor and the American Community* (Simon and Schuster, 1970).

Boulding, Kenneth E., *Economics as a Science* MacGraw-Hill, 1970).

Bower, Joseph L., *Managing the Resource Allocation Process* (Irwin, 1972).

Blake, Robert R., and Mouton, Jane S., *The Managerial Grid* (Houston: Gulf Publishing Co., 1964).

Broden, P., 'Turbulence and Organizational Change.' Linköping Studies in Science and Technology. Dissertation N. 7, 1976.

Chandler, A. D., Jr. *Strategy and Structure* M. I. T. Press, 1972).

Channon, D., 'Corporate Strategy and Organizational Structure in British Industry's, *Journal of Business Policy*, No. 3, 1972.

Clausewitz, Karl von, *On War* (9th Edn.) (Routledge, 1968).

Cordiner, Ralph, J., *New Frontiers for Professional Managers* (McGraw-Hill, 1956).

Cooper, William W., Leavitt Harald J. and Shelly M. W., *New Perspectives in Organizational Research.* (Wiley, 1964).

Crozier, M., 'Le problème de l'innovation dans les organizations économiques', *Sociologie du Travail*, Vol. 10, January–March 1968.

Crozier, M., 'Les problèmes humains que posent les structures de l'enterprise dans une societé en changement.' Paper presented at Cannes Colloquium, March 1971.

Cyert, Richard M., and March, James G., *A Behavioral Theory of the Firm* (Prentice-Hall, 1963).

Drucker, Peter F., *The Age of Discontinuity* (Harper and Row, 1969).

De Brugne, P., 'Esquisse d'une théorie de l'administration des entreprises', *Librairie Universitaire*, Louvain, 1963.

De Woot, Ph., *La Fonction d'enterprise: formes nouvelles et progrès économique* (Louvain, Éditions Nauwelaerts, 1962).

Emery, F. E., and Trist, E. L., 'The Causal Texture of Organizational Environments', *Human Relations*, Vol. 18, 1965, pp. 21–32.

Emery, F. E., and Trist E. L., *Towards a Social Ecology: Contextual Appreciation of the Future in the Present* (Plenum Press, 1973).

Etzioni, Amitai, *Modern Organizations* (Prentice-Hall, 1967).

Forrester, J. W., *Industrial Dynamics* (MIT Press, 1961).

Friedman, Milton, *Capitalism and Freedom* (Chicago University Press, 1962).

Galbraith, J. K., *The Affluent Society*, 2nd Edn. (Houghton Mifflin, 1969).

Galbraith, J. K., *Designing Complex Organizations* (Addison-Wesley, 1973).

Hertzberg, Frederick, *Work and the Nature of Man* (World Publishing, 1970).

Heyvaert, Hubert, *Stratégie et innovation dans l'entreprise* (Université Catholique de Louvain, 1973).

Hodgkinson, Harold L. *Institutions in Transition* (McGraw-Hill, 1970).

Jay, Anthony, *Management and Machiavelli* (Holt, Rinehart, 1967).

Kast Fremont E., and Rosenzweig, James E., *Organizations and Management: A systems Approach* (McGraw-Hill, 1970).

Katz, D., and Kahn, R. L., *The Social Psychology of Organizations* (Wiley, 1966).

Koontz, Harold, 'The Management Theory Jungle', *Academy of Management Journal*, 4, December 1961, pp. 174–188.

Lawrence, P. R., and Lorch, J. W., *Organization and Environment* (Harvard Business School, 1967).

Leavitt, Harold, *Managerial Psychology* (University of Chicago Press, 1965). (*See* Ch. 26: Technology and Organization.)

Levinson, H., *The Exceptional Executive: A Psychological Conception* (Harvard University Press, 1968).

Levinson, H., *Organizational Diagnosis* (Harvard University Press, 1972).

Likert, Rensis, *New Patterns of Management* (McGraw-Hill, 1961).

Lindblom, C. E., *The Intelligence of Democracy* (New York: Free Press, 1965).

Lindblom, C. E., *The Policy Making Process* (Prentice-Hall, 1968).

Lodge, George C., *The New American Ideology* (Knopf, 1975).

Lorange, P., 'Tailoring the Capital Budgeting System to the Behavioral Style of Management', Doctoral Thesis, Harvard Business School, 1971.

MacGregor, Douglas, *The Human Side of Enterprise* (McGraw-Hill, 1969).

Machiavelli, Niccolo, *The Prince* (Penguin Books).

Maier, Norman R., *Problem-Solving Discussions and Conferences: Leadership Methods and Skills*, (McGraw-Hill, 1973).

Mansfield, Edwin, *Microeconomics* (2nd Edn.) (Norton, 1975).

March, J. G., and Simon, H. A., *Organizations* (Wiley, 1958). (*See* Ch. 5: Conflict in Organizations.)

Maslow, Abraham H., *Motivation and Personality* (Harper and Row, 1954).

Miller, R. E., 'Innovation, Organization and Environment.' (Université Catholique de Louvain, *Nouvelle Série No. 86*, 1971).

Mintzberg, H., 'Strategy Making in Three Modes', *California Management Review*, 1973).

Myrdal, Gunnar, *Against the Stream: Critical Essays on Economics* (Pantheon Books, 1963).

Normann, Richard, *Management and Statesmanship* (Siar, 1976).

Pettigrew, A. M., *The Politics of Organizational Decision Making* (Tavistock, 1973). (*See* Ch. 9: Sources and Use of Power in Decision Process).

Raiffa, H., *Decision Analysis*, (Addison-Wesley, 1970).

Rothschild, William E., *Putting It all Together: A Guide to Strategic Thinking* (American Management Association, 1976).

Selznick, P., 'Foundations of the Theory of Organizations', *American Sociological Review*, Vol. 13, 1948.

Selznick, P., *Leadership in Administration* (Harper and Row, 1957).

Scheiffer, F., 'Planning for the Unexpected', *McKinsey Quarterly*, Spring 1974.

Scott, B. R., *Stages of Corporate Development* (Harvard Business School, 1970).

Silk, Leonard, and Vogel, David, *Ethics and Profits* (Simon and Schuster, 1976).

Sloan, Alfred P., Jr. *My Years with General Motors* (Doubleday, 1964).

Smith, Adam, *The Wealth of Nations*, 1776, (Chapter IV: How the Towns Improve the Country).

Steiner, George A., *Top Management Planning* (Riverside, N. J. Macmillan, 1969).

Thomas, J. M., and Bebnis, W. G., *Management of Change and Conflict* (Penguin Books, 1972).

Thompson, James D., *The Behavioral Sciences: An Interpretation* (Addison-Wesley, 1970).

Thompson, James D., *Organizations in Action* (MacGraw-Hill, 1967) (*See* Ch. 2: Rationality in Organization; Ch. 8, The variable Human).

Vernon, Raymond, *Sovereignty at Bay* (2nd Edn.) (New York: Basic Books, 1972).

Vroom, V., and Yetton, P., *Leadership and Decision Making* (University of Pittsburgh Press, 1973).

Wagle, B., 'The Use of Models for Environmental Forecasting and Corporate Planning', *Operational Research Quarterly*, Vol. 20, pp. 327–36.

Whitehead, A. N., *The Function of Reason* (Beacon Press, 1958).

Zaleznik, Abraham, 'Power and Politics in Organized Life', *Harvard Business Review*, Vol. 48, May–June 1970.

Zaleznik, A., and Kets de Uries, M.F.R., *Power and the Corporate Mind* (Houghton Mifflin, 1975).

Index